MYSTERIES AND LEGENDS

OF MONTANA

TRUE STORIES
OF THE UNSOLVED AND UNEXPLAINED

ED LAWRENCE

TWODOT®

GUILFORD, CONNECTICUT
HELENA, MONTANA
AN IMPRINT OF THE GLOBE PEQUOT PRESS

To buy books in quantity for corporate use
or incentives, call **(800) 962–0973**
or e-mail **premiums@GlobePequot.com.**

A · TWODOT® · BOOK

Copyright © 2007 Morris Book Publishing, LLC

All rights reserved. No part of this book may be reproduced or transmitted in any form by any means, electronic or mechanical, including photocopying and recording, or by any information storage and retrieval system, except as may be expressly permitted by the 1976 Copyright Act or by the publisher. Requests for permission should be made in writing to The Globe Pequot Press, P.O. Box 480, Guilford, Connecticut 06437.

TwoDot is a registered trademark of Morris Book Publishing, LLC.

Text design by Lisa Reneson, Two Sisters Design

Library of Congress Cataloging-in-Publication Data
Lawrence, Ed.
  Mysteries and legends of Montana / Ed Lawrence. — 1st ed.
    p. cm. — (Mysteries and legends series)
  Includes bibliographical references.
  ISBN 978-0-7627-4152-6
  1. Montana—History—Miscellanea. 2. Montana—Miscellanea. I. Title.
  F731.6.L39 2007
  978.6—dc22

                                                      2007003731

Manufactured in the United States of America

TABLE OF CONTENTS

PREFACE

Before considering the mysteries and legends that lie between the covers of this book, you might want to suspend your preconceived notions about the nature of reality. Try to take these small bits and pieces of information (some of which require, admittedly, a leap of faith) at face value. Consider that, as far as we know, no one involved in any of these mysteries or legends is (or was) attempting to perpetrate a hoax.

For instance, when former Deputy Dan Campbell says that he saw dead cows in trees, we should try to believe him. After all, he grew up on a Montana ranch and was, at one point, a livestock inspector. Dan knows a cow when he sees one. And when members of the law enforcement community and the United States Air Force agree on the presence of unidentifiable craft occupying the space overhead, maybe their observations are worth a second look. In addition, consider a closer examination of the ghost towns Bannack and Virginia City even though these days the streets are pretty civilized, filled with browsing tourists.

It's easy to forget that in the 1860s these same streets were filled with prospectors looking for their fortunes and scoundrels (perhaps even the sheriff) interested in separating the prospectors from their money.

Lest there be any confusion, we're not trying to convince you that any of these mysteries and legends are real. But since it is mostly impossible to prove a negative (like the nonexistence of a monster living in Flathead Lake), how about we just agree that some of these mysteries are, well, pretty darn mysterious?

So sit down with this small sampling of tales from Big Sky Country and, if nothing else, let yourself be entertained. Forge ahead. Turn the page. Have fun.

CHAPTER ONE

WHAT HAPPENED TO MERIWETHER'S BOAT?

Should you decide to engage in a Montana treasure hunt along the Missouri River near Great Falls, Ken Karsmizki believes there's a chance you may unearth a 38-foot boat that once belonged to Meriwether Lewis.

Here's the background: Not long after the United States declared its independence from King George, Jefferson and his fellow newcomers to this land of opportunity began looking to the western horizon for new places to explore. Since most of the area west of the Appalachians belonged to foreigners, this meant some international wheeling and dealing. The end result? The Louisiana Purchase.

According to an agreement made with France and signed on April 30, 1803, for the bargain price of $15 million, the United States bought two million square miles of land, stretching from the Mississippi River to the Rocky Mountains. After the Senate ratified the deal on October 20, 1803, the Spanish, who had never relinquished physical possession of Louisiana to the French, did so in a ceremony at New Orleans. At a second ceremony the French turned the Louisiana Territory over to the United States, and Jefferson had the cat in the bag.

Thirty-year-old Meriwether Lewis, in addition to being a close personal friend to the president, enjoyed a reputation as a bright and inventive individual, an excellent organizer, and a tightfisted manager. When it came time for Jefferson to organize an expedition into the new territory, a "Corps of Discovery," Lewis seemed like a natural choice for leader.

To prepare for his expedition into the new territory, Lewis completed courses in medicine, botany, zoology, and celestial observation. He also studied the journals of those explorers who had preceded him as far west as North Dakota. In June he contacted William Clark, a thirty-three-year-old ex-army lieutenant and skilled river man, geographer, and cartographer with whom he had first become acquainted when he'd been Clark's underling. Clark was offered the position of co-commander, and the expedition was named the "Lewis and Clark Corps of Discovery."

The duo got along famously, perhaps because they were temperamental opposites. Lewis was introverted and moody; Clark was extroverted, even-tempered, and gregarious. The more refined Lewis, who possessed a philosophical, romantic, and speculative mind, was at home with abstract ideas; Clark, the pragmatist, was a man of action. Their relationship ranks high in the realm of notable associations, a rare example of two men sharing responsibilities in a dangerous enterprise without ever losing each other's respect or loyalty.

During the summer before their journey, Lewis oversaw the construction of an iron-framed keelboat he sometimes referred to as "a canoe." The virtue of it would be that it could be collapsed, carried along, and then reassembled as needed. Initial construction took place at Harper's Ferry, West Virginia, but turned out to be a bigger task than anticipated. Lewis wrote, "My greatest difficulty was the frame of the canoe, which could not be completed without my personal attention to such portion of it as would enable the workman to understand the design perfectly. . . ." From his notes we can discern the length of the boat to have been about 38 feet, consisting of six body sections, the stem, and stern.

The armature for the boat was eventually completed and shipped in sections to St. Louis. In the meantime Lewis took passage down the Ohio River, picking up Clark and recruiting expedition members along the way. By fall Camp Wood was established upstream from St. Louis and the corps had settled in for the winter.

On May 14, 1804, the company set off. Their group consisted of approximately forty-five soldiers and boatmen, and Lewis's dog, Seaman. By October they had arrived at the earthlodge villages of the Mandan and Hidatsa Indians, where they settled in for winter number two.

It wasn't until June of the next year that Lewis had occasion to try out his new boat. Scouting ahead of the main body, he caught sight of the anticipated Great Falls of the Missouri. The falls, however, were more extensive than he had expected. He realized that the expedition needed to portage around them. It would take a month.

There was another disappointment in store for him as well. He'd been planning to piece his boat together after the portage, covering the frame with animal skins. He wrote, ". . . Game becoming more abundant this morning and I thought it best now to loose no time . . . in providing the necessary quantity of Elk's skins to cover my leather boat which I now expect I shall be obliged to use shortly. . . ." And later, he added,

> on my arrival at the upper camp this morning, I found that Sergt. Gass and Shields had made but slow progress in collecting timber for the boat; they complained of great difficulty in getting streight or even tolerably streight sticks of 4½ feet long. We were obliged to make use of the willow and box elder, the cottonwood being to soft and brittle. . . . I have found some pine logs among the drift wood near this place, from which, I hope to obtain as much pitch as will answer to pay the seams of the boat. I directed Fraizer to remain in order to sew the hides together, and form the covering for the boat.

Nothing seemed to be going right for Lewis and his boat. He soon discovered that assembling the boat in the unpre-

Captain Meriwether Lewis and Federal Armory Superintendent Joseph Perkins inspect Lewis's assembled iron boat frame.

dictable conditions of the field was going to be much harder than he'd thought. Two weeks later, he wrote:

> This morning I had the boat removed to an open situation, scaffold her off the ground, turned her keel to the sun and kindled fires under her to dry her more expediciously. I set a couple of men to pounding of charcoal to form a composition with some beeswax which we have and buffaloe tallow now my only hope and resource for paying my boat; I sincerely hope it may answer yet I feel it will not. the boat in every other rispect completely answers my

most sanguine expectation; she is not yet dry and eight men carry her with the greatest ease; she is strong and will carry at least 8,000 lbs. With her suit of hands; her form is as complete as I could wish it. The stiches begin to gape very much since she has began to dry;

I am now convinced this would not have been the case had the skins been sewed with a sharp point only and the leather not cut by the edges of a sharp nedle."

Days later, he continued

. . . we corked the canoes and put them in the water and also launched the boat, she lay like a perfect cork on the water, five men would carry her with the greatest ease. I now directed seats to be fixed in her and oars to be fitted. The men loaded the canoes in readiness to depart . . . the wind continued violent untill late in the evening, by which time we discovered that a greater part of the composition had seperated from the skins and left the seams of the boat exposed to the water and she leaked in such manner that she would not answer . . . it was irreparable.

It is a sad day when a man loses his favorite boat. He later wrote:

I therefore relinquished all further hope . . . and ordered her to be sunk in the water, that the skins might become soft in order the better to take her in pieces tomorrow and deposit the iron fraim at this place . . . Had I only singed my Elk skins in stead of shaving them I believe the composition would have remained and the boat have answered at least untill we could have reached pine country . . . where we might have supplyed ourselves with the necessary pich or gum. But it was now too late to introduce a remidy and I bid a dieu to my boat, and her expected services."

The corps headed west to the ocean, and Lewis's pride and joy was left buried on the banks of the Missouri near the present-day city of Great Falls. A Montana mystery was born, the boat's location the subject of an ongoing debate among historians.

When the explorers returned to Montana a year later, they unearthed the leaky vessel. On July 14, 1806, almost exactly one year after the burial, Lewis wrote his final words about the boat, ". . . Had the carriage wheels dug up. Found them in good order. The iron frame of the boat had not suffered materially. . . . "

With no further cataloging from Lewis, the mystery deepened. What finally happened to the boat? Most Lewis and Clark students maintain that the boat must have been reburied, probably somewhere in the vicinity of Great Falls.

But Carl Camp disagrees. An emeritus professor of political science at the University of Nebraska at Omaha and a founding member of the Lewis and Clark Trail Heritage Foundation's Mouth of the Platte Chapter, Camp has written, "Whoa! Hold on to your metal detectors, probes, picks, and shovels. It's highly unlikely that the frame of the iron boat is today anywhere near the site of the Upper Portage Camp. Lewis and Clark aficionados are looking in all the wrong places if they confine their search for the remnants of the iron boat frame to the area around Great Falls."

The frame's fate after it was dug up, he adds, "remains one of the minor mysteries of the expedition. Did Lewis have the parts returned to the cache . . . leave the parts strewn about the site to be washed away in later floods . . . order his men to put the pieces of iron in the river so he would be done with it once and for all? Knowing . . . Lewis's apparently obsessive personality, none of these scenarios seems plausible. Where, then, do we go from here?"

Camp fast-forwards to the expedition's return to the Hidatsa and Mandan Indian villages. He notes that the corps gave its swivel gun, ammo, and blacksmithing tools to Hidatsa Chief Le Borgne. He then hypothesizes that they donated the iron frame to Charbonneau, the Frenchman who was their scout on the journey, since Lewis had declared that he had "lost all further hope" for the boat a year earlier.

Thus, he concludes, the parts of the frame "probably have been long since altered, fragmented, transformed, and, figuratively speaking, scattered to the four winds."

In response, however, John L. Stoner, a respected Lewis and Clark aficionado, has written, "Camp fails to mention that Lewis and his party also took the time to dig up several caches before going to work on the red pirogue," a canoe in need of repair. "I doubt the explorers removed the red pirogue's nails because they wanted to use them for trade with the Indians. Instead, they probably wanted them for repairs to the white pirogue, which had seen hard usage during the trip. . . . For my money, I'll stick with Karsmizki's theory."

The aforementioned Ken Karsmizki is generally considered the preeminent archeologist of Lewis and Clark sites. During his tenure at Bozeman's Museum of the Rockies, he spent twelve years researching the travels of the corps before, in 1998, conclusively pinpointing the location of the Lower Portage Camp 10 miles northeast of Great Falls. He was also successful in identifying Lewis and Clark's Fort Clatsop at the mouth of the Columbia River.

Karsmizki's response to Camp appeared in a November 2004 issue of *We Proceeded On,* the official publication of the Lewis and Clark Trail Heritage Foundation. The title was, "Lewis's Iron Boat (An Alternative to Carl Camp's Hypothesis)." And the gauntlet was thrown down.

Karsmizki wrote, "When Lewis returned to the Upper Portage Camp he ordered the frame dug up, and then either reburied (my view) or transported downstream (Camp's view). Others argue that the boat was buried but discovered by Indians.

Though Indians did find two caches that were exposed by river conditions there is no evidence of Indians discovering any other expedition cache." He believes Lewis and Clark reburied the boat because fewer than half of the party's complement of helpers was available to transport the bulk of equipment and supplies over the 20-mile portage route around the Great Falls.

Camp contends that "they had more cargo room on the return than on the trip west." To this Karsmizki replies, "In fact, they left in 1805 with eight dugout canoes and returned a year later with six, one of which they abandoned."

Karsmizki continues, "If, as Camp and others argue, the destitute explorers intended to use the iron for trade one would expect them to look forward to unearthing the frame with the greatest anticipation. Yet, Lewis's journal entry says nothing about its potential trade value but merely notes, in the most matter of fact way, that it 'had not suffered materially'." Of others' contention that the nails were scavenged for trade purposes, Karsmizki says, "I believe the evidence from the journals shows that the explorers chiefly valued nails for their versatility in making repairs." He continues, "One might reasonably ask, 'Why did the explorers open the cache in the first place?' Well, it seems Lewis had stored some papers and other small items in the boat, so one can reasonably assume that the captain wanted to retrieve these papers."

Camp's response? "I believe most of the arguments he [Karsmizki] advances in favor of the (Upper Portage) site are off base or just plain wishful thinking." Of the cargo-carrying capacity of the flotilla he writes, "The downstream flotilla had to accommodate only one half of the thirty-two members of the expedition because twelve members, including Clark, were more than 100 miles away on the Yellowstone River."

Enter into the debate Vic Reiman, a Lewis and Clark buff at the Montana Historical Society. In building his argument that the iron frame of the boat must have been traded to the Indians, Reiman points out that the 1806 portage of the Great Falls "was accomplished by 16 men, two teams of horses, and two low wagons or carts." (No horses were used on the portage the previous year.)

Reiman wrote, "Although Lewis told the portagers that he would meet them at the mouth of the Marias no later than the 5th of August, the men arrived at the Marias on July 28th . . . On July 28, when Lewis met his men on the Missouri above the Marias, he reported in his journal that all things had been brought safe: '. . . I now learned that they had brought all things safe having sustaned no loss nor met with any accident of importance. . . .'"

Reiman continued, "Neither Captain Lewis, nor Sergeant Gass, nor Sergeant Ordway reported in their journals that the boat frame had been abandoned (or reburied)." Later on the same day of their surprise reunion on the river, they all did report their inability to locate a cache with several beaver traps. Lewis and Ordway also recorded the loss through water damage of some beaver pelts and a robe in a cache near the mouth of the

Marias. The same day Lewis even recorded the loss due to water damage of some parched meal in a cache.

Reiman wrote, "Iron was extremely valuable as a trade item with the Indians. At Fort Mandan they had traded a 4" square from a burnt out sheet iron stove for 7 or 8 gallons of corn. . . . Although on July 28, 1806, they were apprehensive that the Blackfeet might have been pursuing them, they took the time at the mouth of the Marias to remove all the iron work (including nails) from the red pirogue, which was rotted out. They also recovered the blacksmith tools they had cached the previous year.

"I believe that Lewis buried his boat frame in 1805 with the intention of recovering it on the return trip and making it work right at some future time. Lewis wrote a detailed analysis of the reasons for the failure of his 'favorite boat' and suggested ways in which the iron frame boat might be successfully assembled in the future. If it were his intention to simply abandon the boat frame he could have accomplished that without the effort of taking it to pieces and securing it in its cache. With the current of the Missouri River to do the work, all that would have been required to deliver the boat frame to St. Louis would have been to carry it back over the portage and load it into a boat. The boat frame is estimated to have weighed about 200 lbs. and it would have been a simple matter to have loaded it into one of the canoes drawn on a cart by a team of horses. The boat was portaged up to White Bear in 1805 by simply placing it in one of the canoes on a cart drawn by men. To men who were used to carrying large quantities of meat over land back to their camps, 200 lbs. would not have been an unmanageably heavy weight."

To back his claim regarding Lewis's accounting methods, Reiman wrote, "Lewis used the common type of inventory keeping system in which items are logged in and out of the inventory. If an item is not mentioned one must assume that it has had no change in status. Once an item is logged in it is not necessary to keep repeating the status of that item. Some scholars argue that Lewis's dog, Seaman, did not complete the journey because he was no longer mentioned after a certain point in Lewis's journal. I think it is safe to suppose that Lewis would have recorded the loss of his beloved Seaman and, likewise, if the frame of his 'favorite boat' had been carelessly abandoned, Lewis would have recorded it."

In an interview in 2006, Karsmizki maintained simply, "They buried the boat because they didn't need it to go home." Karsmizki remains convinced that the boat is buried somewhere near Great Falls. "But the river is not stable and meanders, perhaps away from the burial site. Or, it could have been buried on an area that is now covered by a subdivision."

Either way, he says, "We still have not exhausted all of the possibilities."

Surprisingly, though the debate sounds acrimonious on paper, all of the participants agree that while the world of historical research is rife with disagreements, these debates are healthy. For his part Camp hopes that Karsmizki will eventually find the frame, despite believing that he's looking in the wrong place.

CHAPTER TWO

A MUMMY AND THE LITTLE PEOPLE

The most prominent remains of a Little Person were discovered by gold prospectors in a cave in northern Wyoming in 1932. The tiny corpse was found in a sitting position, cross-legged with its hands folded in its lap. A macabre Buddha, he appeared to have been middle-aged when he died, his skin dark brown and wrinkled, his nose flat and splayed, the forehead low, the mouth thin lipped and wide. But he was only 14 inches tall. At the time, puzzled scientists ventured that it might have been a mummified pygmy, possibly the progenitor of the American Indian. They concluded that it had been given a ceremonial burial.

Naturally, a discovery of this type captured the public's attention. The mummy became an object of interest in sideshows for several years before it was purchased by Ivan T. Goodman. Goodman took it to New York City for examination and X-rays performed by Dr. Harry Shapiro of the American Museum of Natural History. The mummy then went to Boston where it was eventually confirmed as being an authentic mummy by the

Anthropology Department of Harvard University. The remains were considered to be those of a sixty-five-year-old person. Attention was drawn to the legends of the local Native Americans. Were the Northern Plains tribes right in their belief in the existence of a race of Little People?

Following Goodman's death in 1950, the mummy disappeared into the hands of a second party, though interest in it continued. In 1979 pictures of Shapiro's X-rays were given to Dr. George Gill, a professor of anthropology at the University of Wyoming. The withered little body, he concluded, was that of an infant or a fetus, possibly of an unknown tribe of prehistoric Indians. He believed that the infant had been afflicted with anencephaly, a congenital abnormality that would account for the adult proportions of its skull.

But there's more.

Area tribes considered the Pryor Mountain and Wind River country of southern Montana and northern Wyoming to be the center of the universe for the Little People. If the legends are true, it shouldn't be surprising, then, that certain, unexplainable discoveries have been made from time to time. During the first half of the twentieth century, a local attorney on a fishing trip to Pathfinder Dam discovered a small human corpse in a cavern. The mummified remains were only about 20 inches tall. Along about the same time, a Mexican sheepherder discovered a small mummy and six skulls in the same vicinity. In the 1940s a small corpse was set on display in a station wagon and put on a money-making tour of college campuses. For 25 cents you could take a look at it.

Interestingly enough, the legends aren't restricted to just one or two tribes. The oral histories of many different Native peoples described the presence of a race of tiny people. Sometimes the stories cast the creatures in a friendly, benevolent light, while other times the Little People were portrayed as being mischievous—more like juvenile delinquents. Some tribes called them "Stick Indians" because they lived in the woods; others called them the "Little People." Apart from their size, they looked like typical humans. Their wardrobe usually consisted of deer- and goatskins wrapped tightly around their tiny bodies. The Nez Perce called them *Its'te-ya-ha* and said they lived deep in the woods. They believed that the Little People would occasionally rub themselves with certain types of grass to make themselves invisible.

Among certain tribes of western Montana, it was forbidden to discuss the Little People or reveal their stories. It was believed that the tellers could be injured by the spirit powers. An old Kalispel medicine man named Charlie Gabe, however, once told anthropologist H. H. Turney-High of a time during his youth when he ascended a mountain on a spirit quest. Seeking unusual power, he chose to climb the highest peak in the area. Nearing a lake, he saw white muskrats, among the Indians a sign that his efforts would be rewarded. Nearing the summit of the mountain, he discovered a freshly cut cottonwood log, totally out of place on the peak, belonging as it did to the valleys thousands of feet below. Feeling that the spirit was close at hand, he ascended to the summit where he found a large hole. Looking into the hole, he saw a group of Little People beginning to dance. When they discovered him, he was invited by the chief to join the festival. The celebration continued for four nights. The days were spent recovering from the ordeal. When he left, he attempted to take one of the Little People with him, but his efforts were unsuccessful.

One pioneer in the Wind River country apparently came upon several ancient dwellings made of sticks and stones and held together by mud. He was told by older Indians that the abodes had been constructed before the arrival of the local tribes and were homes of the Ninnimbe, or "Little Demons." He was told these "demons" were 2 or 3 feet high, strong and fearless. They wore clothing of goatskins and carried large quivers filled with arrows. They were stealthy stalkers, expert hunters, and good fighters. They were reputed to have killed early Shoshone using invisible, poison arrows.

Included in the Indian lore of the period are stories of Little People having made drawings on rocks and carvings that talked at night. Admiring the pictures angered the Little People, but relief from their ire could be accomplished by donning war paint, which they feared.

The Shoshone also believed that if a man became ill or his horse went lame or even if his wife ran away with another man,

E. J. BASHOR

Rumors regarding a race of "little people" in the mountains of the West have been fortified by discoveries of mysterious mummies, like this twenty-inch-tall specimen discovered in a Wyoming cave.

these misfortunes could be blamed on the Little People and their invisible arrows.

A popular tale from the Pryors involves a child who fell from a travois only to be kidnapped and raised in a cave by the Little People. The lad stayed with his kidnappers until he became a man of superhuman strength. As told by the Crow Indians, he went on to build hundreds of piles of rocks in the Pryor Mountains. His biggest construction, called Medicine Rock, became home to the Little People.

To the Crow Indians, the Little People were protectors. Whether they existed as spirits or as flesh and blood seemed of little importance to this tribe. Stories are still told of how, during the days of intertribal warfare, the Little People would ambush the war parties of Crow enemies, tearing the hearts from the enemies' horses.

In a medicine dream Plenty Coups, the famous Crow chief, was led through the air from a high mountain by a spirit person who took him to a lodge filled with warriors of various, unfamiliar nations. He was shown that they were bad warriors intent on bringing evil into the world. With this knowledge Plenty Coups was able to avoid these miscreants.

Shirley Smith, owner of the Little Cowboy Bar and Museum in Fromberg, Montana, has been in pursuit of Little People history since she saw a mummy in school at age seven. Though personally having come close to a Little Person encounter on only one occasion, she has compiled a detailed library of Little People stories and anecdotes. She also numbers among her acquaintances at least one person who has had a visitation.

Among her historical documents is the story of two cowboys who, after being on the trail for three days, settled in around a campfire for the night. When one of them awoke to check the fire, he found that he and his sidekick were surrounded by a band of people that were no more than 3 feet tall. He didn't mention the visitation until, weeks later, a similar event was recounted by another cowboy.

Some tribal members also believe that the Little People can take on animal form, which fits with the story of Carson Yellowtail. During the winter of 1906, he and a friend were snowshoeing in the wilderness backcountry when his friend took ill. As Carson began snowshoeing out for help, he soon noticed that a wolflike or coyote-like animal was following close behind. The animal soon came so close that he occasionally brushed up against Carson. It was apparently herding him in a particular direction. At one point the animal kept Carson from falling over a precipice. When Carson finally reached a ranch house, the animal disappeared. Was it a Little Person in animal form?

Richard Myers, an acquaintance of Shirley Smith, recounted an incident that happened while he was attending a Mountain Man Rendezvous in the MacDonald Basin of the Absaroka Mountains. "During the event, Hash McDonald began playing flute music in an attempt to call the Little People," he said. At evening's end, the pair left a tobacco offering in their tepee, a common gift for Indian spirits. "Then strange stuff began happening. The emergency flashers on my truck began flashing, and I couldn't turn them off. For no reason, the valve of an oil tank several feet above the ground had been mysteriously opened and oil was being spilled. And we heard voices outside the tepee but weren't able to find any tracks." He also reported seeing a bright yellow light moving near the campsite, the origin of which was unexplainable. Myers was convinced that it was the Little People and that they are "rascals who like to mess around with vehicle lights."

On a separate occasion, during a spring bear hunt, he and his companions doused a campfire that they had built in a medicine ring. Upon their return a week later, they found the fire had been restarted, but there was no one in the vicinity.

Shirley Smith tells of traveling with four acquaintances to a picnic on the lower edge of the Pryor Mountains at noon on a sunny summer day. When they arrived at the deserted picnic site, they found a freshly constructed fire waiting for them (not what you might expect in the summertime). "But there were no other people around," she said.

She also spins the tale of an episode that involved an uncle who ranches in the Pryor Mountains. While he was digging an irrigation ditch with his tractor, a section of dirt collapsed, revealing a large cave. Returning to the site with a lantern, he discovered that three sides of the cave were filled with dirt shelves lined with the petrified mummies of Little People. Out of respect for the deceased, he covered up the cave and now refuses to divulge its location.

Most Indians in the area generally maintain that the Little People left southern Montana in the 1890s, their departure likely caused by the commotion of railroad and dam construction.

But they may have come back.

In 1991 two members of the Crow Tribe living near the reservation confided to Rich Pittsley, former manager of Plenty Coups State Park, that they may have experienced a sighting. They were surveying a shallow cave in a spiritual area near the reservation when one woman took a lunch break. While she was seated near the cave, "A small man appeared. He was about three feet in height, powerfully built, and dressed in the old ways with traditional hide clothing." When she finished her lunch, the Little Person disappeared, but she and an acquaintance decided it was appropriate to make an offering with prayers and food.

In 1998, while driving along the reservation's two-lane road, a Crow woman saw what appeared to be a small man wearing an Elvis Presley–style outfit. He was pushing a wheelbarrow along the road. She thought she was just so tired that she was seeing things. But then later that day, her sister, while making the same drive, saw the same man. When they discussed the events with others, they learned that a nearby farmer had become quite frustrated at the disappearance of his wheelbarrows.

Whether these appearances are real or imagined, elaborate hoaxes or honest (if unexplainable) events, it's almost impossible to say for certain. But given how the Little People have put in appearances in the histories of so many different, often divergent, tribes and given how their small bodies keep showing up, they're almost impossible to dismiss out of hand. For such a little people, they sure create a big stir.

CHAPTER THREE

DID GOVERNOR MEAGHER GO SWIMMING?
OR WAS HE DROWNED?

The last time anyone saw General Thomas Francis Meagher, he was either floating, thrashing, or swimming in the Missouri River at Fort Benton late on the evening of July 1, 1867. How and why he ended up in the river has been a matter of conjecture for more than 140 years.

Upon his arrival at Fort Benton on that fateful day, the general was a guest for dinner (a midday meal in those days) at the home of I. G. Baker, a businessman with an office across the street from the steamer landing. Later in the day Meagher wrote a letter to his wife and then wandered the streets, eventually arriving at the dock where he boarded the steamer *G.A. Thomson* to spend the night.

According to Baker, at about 10:00 P.M., a company watchman discovered a man struggling in the river. Baker called for help. A group gathered along the bank looking for the late-night swimmer. In the meantime the watchman determined that General

MONTANA HISTORICAL SOCIETY, HELENA

A Civil War general and territorial governor, Thomas Meagher led a tumultuous, controversial life, aspects of which perhaps contributed to his death.

Meagher's stateroom was empty. By this time the swimmer was gone, and the crowd was already dispersing. Fifty yards downstream from the *G.A. Thompson,* another steamer was tied up. Had the man struggling in the water been the general? Had he been swept under the downstream steamer? In any case no body was ever found, and the general was missing.

Considering the number of murders, robberies, Indian attacks, and other unsavory events that occurred on the western frontier during that era, the death of one person, even a general, would not have typically been an unusual occurrence, even if he had possibly been murdered.

But Meagher was also a self-promoting scoundrel who had already become a colorful part of Montana history. His resume listed time spent as an Irish revolutionary and exile, Civil War general, Montana Territorial secretary and acting governor, eloquent lecturer, and all-around rabble-rouser. His story continues to attract interest, especially in the context of his unexplained death.

Unlike most of the thousands who immigrated to the United States from the British Isles, Meagher came from an aristocratic family. He was born in Waterford, Ireland, in August of 1823 and educated at Clongowes Wood, a Jesuit college. Later he attended Stonyhurst College in Lancashire, England. He joined the Irish Youth Movement and became enough of a rabble-rouser in denouncing the Crown that, in 1848, he was arrested and charged with high treason against Her Majesty.

Undaunted by the fact that he had been found guilty, he told the judge, "Your honor, this is our first offense, but not our last. If you will be easy with us this once, we promise, on our word as gentlemen, to try to do better next time. And next time—sure we won't be fools and be caught."

He and nine other members of the student group were eventually banished to Tasmania, the first stop on a route that would lead him to Montana. The penal system being what it was in those days, he was paroled with the understanding that he would remain on good behavior and make no attempt to leave the island. Interestingly, of the nine convicted, one eventually became prime minister of Australia; Meagher was appointed the acting governor of Montana; two became brigadier generals in the United States Army; another became governor general of Newfoundland; another attorney general of Australia; and two were elected to Parliament in Montreal.

In Tasmania Meagher married a local lass and bought a farm where he toiled unhappily for several months. Tiring of the drudgery, he broke his vows and escaped the island in 1852. A long boat trip later, he found himself in New York City where, though an escaped convict, he was greeted with open arms by the Irish community.

In the coming years he established a reputation as an orator, traveling the country making anti-British speeches. Romantic, handsome, a victim of what many considered British intolerance, he took advantage of every political and social connection he found. In New York he was mentored by Judge Robert Emmet, who facilitated Meagher's admission to the legal profession, despite Meagher's lack of training. Much of Meagher's later success is more likely attributed to his wit and charm than to his professional credentials. He began publishing the *Irish News* in 1856 and petitioning the president of the United States that he should be named ambassador to a country in the southern hemisphere, a position for which he also had no apparent credentials.

Along the way he met Elizabeth Townsend, a member of a prominent New York family. They married, over the objections of her father, who reluctantly arranged to have the ceremony conducted in a private service at the residence of the archbishop of New York, thus avoiding the society pages.

In retrospect it seems that every step Meagher took was destined to lead him west. He was young, wild of spirit, impetuous, and self-serving, but at some level he also displayed the character of one bent on public service.

By 1860 Meagher's newspaper and legal practice were both foundering. After a brief detour to Central America, where he'd been hired by a Philadelphia shipping magnate intent on building a transit route across Panama, Meagher decided to use the Civil War as a political stepping-stone. After President Lincoln's call for volunteers, Meagher endeared himself to the White House by recruiting an all-Irish contingent for the Union. He was soon named a colonel in the Sixty-ninth Infantry.

Despite that brief success his military and political fortunes soon spiraled down. After the war, unable to draw crowds to a lecture hall, he began petitioning allies for a political position. He had his eye specifically on the governorship of the Territory of Montana. He also petitioned the War Department for an appointment as major general of the territory, just in case his political appointment was not forthcoming.

On August 3, 1865, a day after delivering a lecture in St. Paul, Minnesota, he was offered the secretaryship of the military in Montana Territory, a position turned down by two others. He arrived in Virginia City, Montana, via stagecoach, after a six-week journey.

The territory was still very wild. More than three hundred road agents were known to circulate among the populace of Virginia City; a group of vigilantes had taken it upon themselves to interpret the workings of the legal system; and the threat of Indian attacks was a fact of daily life. There also were political considerations to be dealt with, some of which eventually led to Meagher's downfall.

Meagher discovered that regional political power was mostly in the hands of Wilbur Fisk Sanders and a group of Republicans appointed by Congress. When confronted with situations that did not work to their favor, Sanders et al. were quick to request assistance from their cronies in the nation's capital. On the other side of the fence were the Southerners, primarily Democrats, who even while holding elected offices, generally looked upon themselves as the oppressed.

Territorial Governor Sidney Edgerton was fed up with the West. He'd had his bags packed for a return to Ohio even before Meagher's arrival. After the elected governor's resignation, the Irishman was immediately promoted from military secretary to acting governor. Republicans scornfully dubbed him "the Acting One."

Before hitting the trail, the previous governor was kind enough to share some facts of life with the newcomer: "There is no hope for your being appointed permanent governor because you are considered a Southern Democrat, despite your loyalty to the north during the Civil War. . . . You will have three enemies. The Sioux Indians, led by Red Cloud, the bravest, most vicious, cunning savage in the Indian nation who is bent on removing the white men from Montana. The Vigilantes. As a group they have gotten out of hand after cleaning up Alder Gulch and Rattlesnake Creek." And, "in your case, the Republicans." Sanders—both a Republican and an organizer of the Vigilantes—concluded: "There is no place right now on God's green earth that is rougher."

After this cheery introduction to his new home, the Acting One began his short stint as chief executive of the territory. Despite the backstabbing environment, he began to work in earnest, becoming something of a pen pal with the president. He petitioned Washington to appoint a surveyor general, requested the establishment of a postal system, and begged for an appropriation for executive and legislative offices, and the payment of overdue salaries to territorial officers. To defend against Indian uprisings, he proposed the establishment of a military garrison and a cavalry force of at least 850 men.

But Edgerton's prophesy about relations with the Republicans proved to be right. The hackles of his political enemies were raised when, in February 1866, Meagher claimed that it was within his power to convene a convention for the purpose of applying for statehood. Meagher may have had his eye on a United States Senate seat. But Sanders traveled to Washington, D.C., where he successfully convinced Congress that such an assemblage was unconstitutional. That was the first time in American history that Congress took unilateral action contrary to the legislative authority of a territory.

An unfriendly territorial judge also declared the convocation of Meagher's legislature a bogus act, his decision effectively writing *finis* to Meagher's first attempts toward Montana statehood.

Almost by accident Meagher also managed to incur the wrath of the Vigilantes. Having sprung up in the absence of legitimate law enforcement, this group of self-appointed executioners dealt unmercifully with suspected criminals. Their unauthorized, speedy trials were mostly conducted in the outdoors, close to trees, and with ropes.

In one incident a cowboy named Jim Daniels had enjoyed a lucky run at poker. When the drunken loser attempted to kill him, Daniels responded by killing the other man first. At the end of the skirmish, he hollered, "I'm innocent!" to a crowd of bystanders. Unknown to Daniels, that was a bad choice of words, since a local gang of highwaymen also allegedly used the same phrase to identify each other. The Vigilantes wrongly assumed Daniels to be a member of this disreputable group, and they took matters into their own hands by tossing him into jail.

Given the testimony of thirty witnesses who said that Daniels was innocent, Meagher commuted the cowboy's sentence and ordered him released. Not smart enough to leave well enough alone, Daniels returned to the saloon for a drink before leaving town. He was again apprehended by the Vigilantes. This time, however, he was strung up. A note pinned to the decedent's jeans announced that Meagher would be next.

Elsewhere in the territory Red Cloud was deciding he'd had enough of the white man's incursion into his hunting grounds and declared that it was time to eradicate the visitors from the territory. Given that threat, which resulted in the deaths of several settlers, including John Bozeman, Meagher petitioned the Feds for a small army and the guns to support them. After Washington agreed to ship a modest supply of arms to the territory, Meagher and an escort of six militia members traveled from Virginia City to Fort Benton to receive the arms. Coincidentally, while en route, Meagher met the newly appointed territorial governor, Green Clay Smith, another Republican from Ohio, at which point Meagher's title reverted back to general.

It's at this point that the history of Meagher's movements and behaviors becomes inconsistent. What we know for certain is that the former acting governor died in the Missouri River. The circumstances of his disappearance, however, are as cloudy as the river is muddy. The only witness to the event was an African-American barber on the steamboat who claimed that the general had let himself down from the upper to the lower deck and then jumped into the river without a word.

Months later, the crew of a steamer headed upstream reportedly found a body, but it was unidentifiable.

On July 7 the *Helena Tri-Weekly* stated, "He had retired to his stateroom, in which he remained for about ten minutes, when he opened the back door for some purpose, and it is supposed not using proper precaution, fell in. Our correspondent was on board the steamer *Guidon* at the time, which was lying below the *G.A. Thompson,* and heard the plunge, saw his head a moment, and then all was still. Every exertion was made for the recovery of his body but without success, and it is doubtful it will be found."

Here's a different version, from *Contributions to the Historical Society of Montana, Volume Eight:* "Meeting some friends on board, the evening was passed in a convivial manner, the [former acting] governor drinking deeply, and becoming intoxicated, when offended by some meaningless remark he grew angry and excited and charged some of the gentlemen present with desiring to take his life."

Then there was an article published in a 1928 edition of *The Eureka Journal.* "It is agreed by all who have investigated the events leading up to the incident that the general was temporarily mentally deranged." The article also notes his bravery and makes mention of the fact that, since suicide is an act of cowardice, Meagher's death must have been an accident. "He plunged into the water without knowing what he was doing."

Wilbur Fisk Sanders, who was at Fort Benton at the time of Meagher's death, wrote, "The day was intensely hot, and the general and his staff had made a swift and dusty ride from Sun River. General Meagher returned from the fort about dusk, in company with some gentlemen whose names I do not recall. My attention was arrested by abnormally loud conversation, and I saw that it came from General Meagher. It was apparent he was deranged. He was loudly demanding a revolver to defend himself against the citizens of Fort Benton who he declared were hostile to him. . . . Several who joined us sought to allay his fears and to restore to sanity his disturbed mental condition."

Sanders further states the Meagher agreed to retire to his stateroom with the proviso that he would be provided with a revolver. With news of the general's drop into the river, Sanders adds this tidbit: "There was a colored man, one of the men connected with the boat—a barber, I believe—who, replying to my interrogations, said a man had let himself down from the upper to the lower deck and jumped into the river and gone on down stream." He then adds, "The next day some members of the general's staff said to me that we must report that he fell from the boat accidentally, and must not report the mental aberration and not attribute it to that. . . . Those who were with him on the last day of his life will join me, I know, in denying his death could be attributed to a convivial habit. I was with him most of the afternoon, and he was resolutely abstemious."

Johnny Doran, the pilot on the *G.A. Thompson* who had invited the general aboard, recorded that the Vigilantes were awaiting Meagher's arrival that day and that the general had armed himself with Doran's pistols. Doran wrote that Meagher had claimed, "very excitedly," that there had been threats to his life.

Doran then convinced Meagher to retire for the evening at about 9:30 P.M.: "I fixed the clothes about him, locked the door of the stateroom, and went down on the lower deck. The lock on the door was defective but I intended to return without delay." Minutes later he heard the sound of a splash and the boat's engineer calling, "Man overboard." Doran later wrote, "The engineer saluted me with, 'It's your friend, Johnny.'"

To complicate matters even further, in 1913 a drunken cowboy known as "Diamond Jack" Miller, during a fit of delirium tremens, confessed to the sheriff of Missoula County that he had killed Meagher. Miller had been a member of the Vigilantes, who were reputed to have carried out more than one contract for murder of cowmen on Rattlesnake Creek. Once sober, however, he recanted his confession.

Murder? Suicide? Accident? One hundred and forty years removed from the incident, we may never know.

CHAPTER FOUR

WAS FRANK LITTLE MURDERED BY A COP?

Butte, Montana, in the early years of the 1900s, was one of the wildest cities in the West. A city of contradictions and conflicts, it was home to both some of the wealthiest capitalists in the world as well as some of the most irate socialists. Few people personified the conflicts of the day so well as Industrial Workers of the World (IWW) leader Frank Little and his nemesis, Sheriff Ed Morrissey. On either side of the labor unrest that roiled through Butte during its boom years, history tends to set the white hat on the head of Little, a wobbly (IWW member) and an Irish immigrant with a reputation for stirring up unrest among the working class. He became something of a martyr on August 1, 1917, when he was murdered by a team of unknown assailants.

The black hat lands on the noggin of Morrissey, who may have worn a badge but was decidedly an all-around bad guy, a disgrace to his honorable profession.

WALTER P. REUTHER LIBRARY, WAYNE STATE UNIVERSITY

Frank Little, a senior member of the Industrial Workers of the World, came to Butte, Montana, looking for recruits. Instead, he found his own mysterious and tragic end.

Understanding the saga of Little and Morrissey requires some knowledge of Butte around the time of World War I. It was a frontier city filled with as many as 100,000 Irish, Scots, Slavs, Italians, and Finns, most of whom had immigrated west in order to earn $4.00 a day—a veritable fortune compared to the $4.00 a month that was common on the Olde Sod—working as miners. At the center of this diverse society was the Anaconda Copper Mining Company (ACM), a monolith controlled by a few autocratic businessmen who considered the working class little more than serfs in their kingdom. ACM was not only the largest employer in the region, but it was one of the largest companies in America.

By 1914 the mining industry was enjoying record profits. Members of the labor unions, however, did not feel they were receiving their fair share of the windfall. They began to organize strikes and protests, seeking better wages and safer working conditions. These actions continually tested the mettle of the police, some of whom were on the payroll of ACM. The police, meanwhile, considered the miners to be anarchists.

There was no middle ground.

The Anaconda Company wielded extraordinary influence on the political, economic, and social environment of the day. Many politicians were owned by the management. The two major newspapers in Butte were also controlled by the Anaconda Company. The resulting "news" reflected what the publishers were, in effect, instructed to print. To counter union activities, the papers were typically lax in reporting news of impending union actions until after the fact, thus defeating miners' attempts to foment change.

Labor unrest began heating up in 1914 when members of the Butte unit of the Western Federation of Miners came to believe that a percentage of the assessments they were sending to aid striking miners in Michigan was not making the journey. They suspected the fees were lining the pockets of the union hierarchy and tavern owners in Butte. They also suspected that union representatives were becoming too cozy with the mining company, as evidenced by the fact that union policy was dictated by ACM. Fractures began to appear in the solidarity of the union ranks when a raucous group of miners disrupted a union parade, vandalized their union hall, and stole the union safe.

Hostilities were further exacerbated in October 1915 when seventeen men were killed by a dynamite explosion in the Speculator Mine.

By 1917 a splinter group representing the radical wing of the International Miners Union formed the Butte Mine Workers Union. The new union's leadership was dominated by the IWW, a far-left, socialist organization determined to foment a revolution.

Among the squeakiest socialist wheels was Frank Little, a union recruiter who traveled from city to city, promoting membership in the IWW. He came to Butte following a stint organizing union members in Arizona. Details of his life before Butte are in short supply, although it was obvious that the fire of unionism burned brightly in his innards. After only eleven years as a member of the IWW, he had risen to membership on the executive board and was the union's designated ambassador of dissent.

A second disaster occurred at the Speculator Mine on June 8, 1917. A fire killed an estimated 164 men, most of them dying from gas inhalation. In response yet another group of miners met four days later to form the Metal Mine Workers Union (MMWU). The companies, however, refused to acknowledge its existence. With the support of the International Brotherhood of Electrical Workers, the miners successfully organized a strike that completely shut down the mines.

At that point the battle lines were drawn between the unions and the Anaconda Company, and the game was afoot. The cops were charged with maintaining the peace.

Prominent among the members of the police officers—and the one perhaps least likely to be voted Butte's Citizen of the Year—was forty-seven-year-old detective, Ed Morrissey.

Like much of Butte's citizenry, Morrissey had been born in Ireland before immigrating to the United States. Not one to stand idle, he volunteered to serve in the Spanish-American War as a member of the First Montana Volunteers. Upon his return to Butte in 1909, he was appointed to the police force. This was during a time when taking bribes was a common practice among police officers. Some police were also known to be in the protection business. It was not uncommon for newspapers to include reports of policemen being investigated for drunkenness, for sleeping on duty—often with prostitutes—or for the excessive use of force. Morrissey was such a success in this atmosphere that he was eventually promoted to the detective division.

Solidifying his reputation as a sympathizer of the mine owners, he made headlines when he conducted an unauthorized raid on a home owned by a reputed socialist union worker. Brandishing a large revolver, he "poured unprintable abuse upon the shirking ears of women and furious ears of men." The chief of police escorted Morrissey from the building before he was able to physically abuse any of its occupants.

Between 1911 and 1917 his misdeeds resulted in his dismissal by a Socialist mayor, then his rehiring by a Democrat, then a suspension for assaulting, with brass knuckles, a former prisoner who had been falsely arrested. The prisoner's only mistake had been in not vacating the premises faster than he could be assaulted. A friendly judge saw no wrongdoing in the cop's methods and ordered his reinstatement. A few days later, however, Morrissey was again suspended for brutalizing a man who was publicly intoxicated, hardly a rarity in the Butte of the time.

The tempers of all participants—miners, mine owners, cops—were wearing thin. And Frank Little was in the midst of it all. The Metal Mine Workers Union apparently disdained the feisty outsider, finding his fiery rhetoric counterproductive to the union's efforts to produce an accord with the mine owners. In fact Tom Campbell, president of the MMWU, pleaded with Little to leave town. Unlike pacifistic union speeches, Little's rants seemed to be advocating violence against ACM's property. This was considered a direct affront to the Anaconda Company.

The MMWU wasn't alone. William Dunne, president of the local chapter of the electricians' union, considered Little, "A very illiterate fellow, not very well informed on labor, who appeared to have a very bitter temperament."

Of note is the fact that in the days before Little's murder, many strike leaders had received threatening letters. Some were nightly changing their sleeping quarters. One IWW leader so feared an outbreak of violence that he left town.

The crime that Morrissey is allegedly responsible and most famous for occurred in the early hours of August 1, when a black convertible carrying a group of thugs parked in front of a boarding house on North Wyoming Street. Among the boarding house's residents was Little.

The masked occupants of the automobile made their way inside, where they announced their presence by breaking down the door to what turned out to be an empty room. Nora Byrne, the landlady, was awakened when the men began an assault on her door. It ceased only when she pointed them to Little's quarters.

In response to a question about their identity, they responded, "We are officers, and we want Frank Little!" It didn't explain their masks, but then nobody in the boarding house wanted any trouble. After kicking in Little's door, the thugs dragged him, clothed only in his undergarments, out to their waiting car. Mrs. Byrne later reported that she had seen none of the men's faces but believed them to be youngish, including one who was "short, chubby, and five feet four inches tall." These were approximately the same dimensions as Morrissey. It took Mrs. Byrne and two other boarders thirty minutes to decide that the episode deserved to be reported to the police.

Witnesses passing outside the boarding house during the fracas described Little being forced into the car, driven several blocks, then pulled from the car and tied to the back bumper, after which he was dragged for four blocks. He was eventually placed back in the car and driven to a railroad trestle behind an old smelter on the southwest side of town where he was unceremoniously hanged.

Shortly before sunrise, while en route to work, Robert Hall discovered the most recent addition to the railroad trestle. A placard attached to the victim's right leg bore the inscription in red crayon, OTHERS TAKE NOTICE. FIRST AND LAST WARNING. 3-7-77. L. D. C. S. S. W. T. The letter T was circled. In Montana's history, the numbers have a grim association, sometimes assumed to mean the dimensions of a grave that would measure 3 feet wide, 7 feet long, and 77 inches deep.

The following morning thousands of Little's friends, many of whom had cheered him at a rally just the day before, paid silent homage during a viewing of his bloody body at the city morgue. Later, 7,000 unionists joined a cortege that accompanied the body of the small man to his final resting place at "The

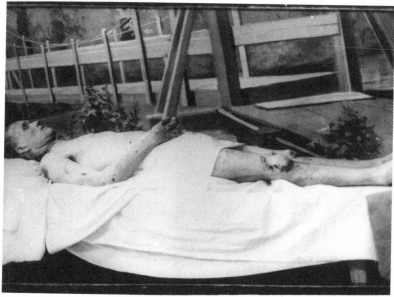

Wobbly recruiter Frank Little was abducted from his boarding house by men claiming to be officers of the law. He was dragged through the streets of Butte before being lynched from a railroad trestle.

Flats," where he joined the company of miners who had died in the shafts, drifts, and stopes beneath Butte.

After the crime MMWU attorney William Sullivan named a laundry list of potential suspects, including "a member of the police force." All of his suspects were employed by the Anaconda Company. Sullivan maintained that the union would pursue justice, but his threat ultimately became idle chatter.

Theories regarding the identity of the perpetrators were in good supply. Little might have been murdered, for instance, by United States soldiers who didn't appreciate his antiwar outbursts. Additionally, folks speculated that he might have been killed by Metal Mine Workers members who were either in need of a martyr since they papered the city with photos of the deceased, or were opposed to his fiery rhetoric. The other rumors implicated the police and the Anaconda Company.

Of Morrissey's possible participation historian Jon Axline wrote, "Morrissey's long affiliations with the company and its hired gunmen make him a likely candidate for the murder of Frank Little." Following one of his dismissals from the force, Morrissey was hired in 1911 as a watchman for ACM, and between 1916 and 1919 drew a salary as chief of detectives while at the same time being on the payroll of ACM. This may explain the city's reluctance to pursue an investigation of Little's murder.

Undeterred by his bad press, Morrissey remained a scourge on the landscape. In 1919 he and a group of ACM guards terrorized voters and polling judges at two city voting spots. In the first, a drunken Morrissey assaulted an innocent visitor to the poll. Later, he assaulted three women ballot judges.

Morrissey's foul behavior continued for the balance of his lifetime. On the home front, he was accused of spousal abuse and the murder of his wife of four months, though the charge was not proven. He was convicted on several accounts of abusing the ladies at the poll and dismissed from the police force. In his last known public fracas he was reportedly involved in a dispute with constable A. C. Hocking, during which both had drawn their guns. Shortly before his death he was involved in a bar fight and was struck on the head by an unidentified assailant wielding a bottle.

The circumstances of Morrissey's death were as unusual as his behavior during life. His frozen body was discovered by his brother, Mike, in Morrissey's lodging at a rooming house on February 3, 1922. According to published reports, his body was only "partially clothed" and in a state of repose, lying sideways on his bed, as if he'd passed out while dressing. Nonetheless, Coroner James Carey ordered an autopsy and inquest. He noted that several bruises and cuts were on Morrissey's chin and face, and an eye had been blackened prior to death.

The coroner found that "the cause of death was pressure of a blood clot on the brain caused by a fall or by being struck by some blunt instrument." Homicide was listed as a possibility—a fitting end for a man known as a first-class scoundrel, drunk, bully, and wife beater.

Lest there be any confusion, the perpetrators of Frank Little's murder were never identified or brought to trial. Although Morrissey was never convicted, his name is atop every list of potential perpetrators.

So technically, the mystery remains. Who did kill Frank Little? Representatives of the mine, who were piqued at the loss of revenue caused by strikes and the potential for more? Members of the army? Members of the MMWU, who saw his presence and actions as a detriment to their efforts? Morrissey and his cohorts?

And who killed Morrissey?

CHAPTER FIVE

IS THE MYSTERY OF THE EASTON MURDER SOLVED?

As long as we are going to have unsolved mysteries in Montana—in this case, murders—we might as well have them two at a time, right?

Take Richard and Alice Easton.

By most accounts the Eastons were an unassuming couple from Iowa who had come to Montana to operate the Paradise Lodge north of Kalispell. Daughter Eleanor described her father as a stubborn former farmer. Sixty-six-year-old Alice was suffering from Parkinson's disease, crippled and unable to walk.

Not long after their arrival, on February 19, 1963, the elderly pair was brutally murdered, their bodies discovered by Eleanor.

Mr. Easton's body was found locked in a garage. "There was blood all over the walls and on the concrete floor," Eleanor said. "He very well could have fought with somebody trying to rob him."

FLATHEAD COUNTY SHERIFF'S OFFICE/PAT WALSH

A Montana murder scene: The Paradise Lodge north of Kalispell

Mrs. Easton had been dragged from her chair near the living-room fireplace and left on the kitchen floor. Investigators at the scene concluded that both victims had been struck repeatedly and their skulls crushed with a sharp object, possibly a tire iron.

They had also been robbed. Eleanor said that her father had kept most of his money in his wallet. The wallet was missing, along with the resort's cash register. The cash register was found several years later in the woods nearby.

The perpetrator left no clues, and the case remained unsolved until 2001 when an unrelated event presented a possible solution. This was when the Royal Canadian Mounted Police discovered a beaten and stabbed body in a frozen creek near Morinville, Alberta. With no suspects in the crime and without even being able to identify the body, the Mounties began circulating photos to law enforcement agencies and the media. Keen-eyed reporter Bill Morlin of Spokane's *Spokesman-Review* identified the deceased as a famous bank robber and escape artist named Kenneth Lloyd Pendleton, a native of Spokane.

Seemingly cut from the same fabric as John Dillinger and Pretty Boy Floyd, Pendleton was known in FBI circles as one of the most slippery and successful bank robbers in America's history. "He's truly a legend in Spokane," said one veteran investigator, speaking off the record. "He's the kind of criminal who commanded a lot of respect from police officers who knew him."

Pendleton was 6 feet tall and over 200 pounds. He once boasted that he could do sixty chin-ups without stopping. His criminal record began not long after his high-school graduation in 1959 when he was convicted of burglary. According to law enforcement officials, he robbed as many as eighty banks in at least eight states, challenging the FBI and law enforcement agencies to a lifelong game of catch-me-if-you-can. When incarcerated, he had a habit of escaping. In one case he somehow used mop strings and abrasive cleaners to saw through prison bars. In another instance he buried himself in a ditch on the grounds of

McNeil Island Prison where, for eleven chilly winter days, he lived off the milk of prison farm cows before swimming to shore. "He's one of a handful that have ever made it off McNeil Island, perhaps the only one during the dead of winter," Federal Probation Officer Bob Banta said at the time.

Back on the street, he was linked to bank robberies in Kettle Falls, Washington, and Pierce, Idaho, before being caught and sentenced to twenty-five years in prison. He escaped from a penitentiary in Bismark, North Dakota, and went on to rob $60,000 from a bank in Glendale, Oregon.

Following his arrest for that crime, he spent the next ten years incarcerated in Oregon. After being released, he is credited with robbing two banks in Spokane. After that his whereabouts were unknown until the discovery of his body.

Detectives from the Flathead County Sheriff's Department traveled to California to interview Pendleton's ex-wife, Arlene LaPierre. During a lengthy interview, Mrs. LaPierre told of being married to Pendleton at the time of the Easton murders and living in a cabin in close proximity to the Paradise Lodge. She had married Pendleton after their senior year in high school.

"And that's when the hell started," she said. "I was held hostage by him for three years or more, usually in backwoods cabins with no phone and no way to get out. In just over three years, we lived in more than twenty places."

Her husband was a thief, and he physically abused her. And then she added that she believed Pendleton was responsible for

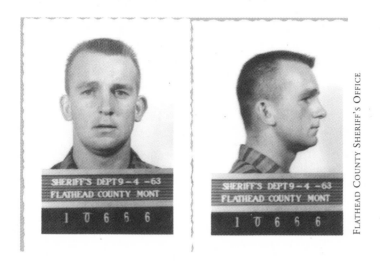

FLATHEAD COUNTY SHERIFF'S OFFICE

Later a victim himself, all clues point to Kenneth Pendleton being the murderer of Richard and Alice Easton.

the 1963 murders. "He returned to our cabin one day covered with blood," she said. "I asked him what happened and he said, 'I hit a deer. Don't ask any more questions.' He took his bloody clothes off, took them outside and burned them. That's the last time we talked about it."

LaPierre had later learned through news reports of the double murder at Paradise Lodge.

Records at the Flathead County jail confirm that Pendleton and LaPierre were in the vicinity at the time of the murders, Pendleton having been booked on a theft charge a few months later.

"We're fairly sure Pendleton is responsible for these homicides," said Maxine Lamb, who was then chief detective of the department. "Mrs. LaPierre told the detectives the same version of events, and added other specific details. Certainly, there will always be a question as to whether or not he really did it, because he's not alive to tell us that he did it. But with the information that has been provided by Arlene LaPierre, we're fairly confident."

But technically we're still left with two unsolved murders. We can assume that Pendleton was responsible for the murders of the Eastons. He had a motive, was in close proximity, and Mrs. LaPierre was a kind of witness. But the detectives have only circumstantial evidence.

And we're still left with the question of who killed Pendleton? And why?

Odds are we'll have to wait for the passage of more time to provide the answer to that question. Or we may never know.

CHAPTER SIX

WAS SHERIFF HENRY PLUMMER A HIGHWAY ROBBER?

A sk most Montana historians about Sheriff Henry Plummer and odds are pretty good that they will either describe him as a villain or a victim. He may have been both. In some eyes, Plummer was a prototypical, if mysterious, law enforcement officer. Others saw him as a wolf in sheep's clothing, living on both sides of the law, using his badge to help him in his crimes.

Regardless, Plummer found a permanent place in Montana's history books when he ran afoul of that infamous group known as the Vigilantes. On the lawless frontier of the 1860s, the Montana Vigilantes were a congregation of gun-toting, rope-slinging, like-minded citizens who decided that they were better administrators of justice than those legally appointed to the task. They were so confident that they managed to get away with hanging Plummer, the sheriff of Bannack, for the commission of crimes for which he had been neither legally charged nor convicted. Plummer was only one of dozens of people accused

55

and executed by this self-righteous bunch. None of its members was ever arrested for what, in some views, were nothing less than murders.

Plummer's Jekyll-and-Hyde profile baffled historians more than a century later. In one view he was known to tip his hat to the ladies, act mannerly, and generally keep to himself.

In another view he was nothing less than a murderer. In a letter to the *Helena Herald,* Judge William Rheem said, "I remember Plummer very well. He was a quiet man and talked but little; when he did speak, it was always in a low tone and with a good choice of language. He never grew boisterous, and no impulse of anger or surprise ever raised his voice above that of a wary monotone. Affection, fear, hate, grief, remorse, or any passion or emotion, found no expression in his immovable face. With mobile and expressive features he would have been handsome—all except for the forehead; this, with the conformation of the skull, betrayed the murders, and Plummer knew it. I have said that Plummer knew he had a bad front; he therefore kept it jealously covered with the turned-down brim of his slouch hat. When he was not in the mood or act of slaughter or rapine, his politeness was notable and well timed."

Gentleman? Or scoundrel with a bad profile? Take your pick. Either way, his downfall began during the days when he lived a seemingly peaceful life as the sheriff of Bannack during a wild time in Montana's history. Bannack and later Virginia City, 70 miles up the road, were the sites of two of the largest gold finds in the West during the 1860s.

The birth of Bannack was strictly an accident. When a group of Colorado miners traveling to the overcrowded gold fields in Lewiston, Idaho, discovered quantities of loose gold along a creek bank, they began scouring the terrain for minerals. As luck would have it, they hit a jackpot. Word of the find spread quickly and miners poured into the area. Historians say that the area eventually produced quantities of gold that, as measured by the acre, rivaled fields in California and Alaska.

Like most mining outposts Bannack quickly became a rough place to live. Imagine muddy unpaved streets filled with crowds of money-hungry men who, in their spare time, had a seemingly insatiable appetite for whiskey, loose women, and cheap food, probably in that order. The smell of easy money also attracted opportunists, some of whom made their money honestly—by selling supplies to the miners, for instance—and others who took their gold at the card tables or at gunpoint.

Considering his history, temperament, and skill with a six-gun, Plummer was a perfect candidate for sheriff in a town looking for someone capable of bringing order to the chaos.

Prior to moving to Montana, Plummer had lived in Nevada City, California, where he'd had his first brush with the law. In that incident, he shot John Vedder, a lodger in Plummer's home. In Plummer's version of the story, Vedder had threatened him with a gun. Plummer shot him in self-defense. Mrs. Vedder initially supported Plummer's story. But then a local newspaper speculated that Plummer might have been motivated by a certain "intimacy between the widow and Plummer." This accusation was never proven, but Mrs. Vedder did later recant her support of Plummer's story. Plummer was convicted of murder and shipped off to San Quentin State Prison.

Eventually pardoned and released, he returned to Nevada City where, during a short stay, he was accused of pistol-whipping one of the locals, murdering William Riley while visiting a house of ill repute, and killing the owner of a dance hall in Oro Fino. Given the prospects of another in stint in prison, Plummer escaped from the local hoosegow and hightailed it north to Montana Territory. He was accompanied by Jack Cleveland, another miscreant.

The duo proceeded to Fort Benton, intending to catch a steamer to St. Louis. But while in Fort Benton, Plummer was smitten by the comely Electa Bryan (as was, not incidentally, Cleveland). Plummer delayed his departure long enough to marry Electa. The newlyweds then decided to settle in Bannack. Shortly after his arrival there, having made a favorable impression on the locals, on May 21, 1963, he was elected sheriff.

In handing the mantle of authority to Plummer, the locals may have, unknowingly, invited the fox into the chicken coop.

It didn't take long for Bannack's newest first citizen to make an impression on his constituents. Cleveland, unhappy at Plummer's besting of him in the courting of Electa, quickly became a weight around the sheriff's neck. He felt he had a modicum of leverage over Plummer by virtue of his knowledge of Plummer's

The grave site of infamous Montana lawman Henry Plummer

Montana Historical Society, Helena

criminal background in California, which was unknown by the Montanans. Cleveland, fortified by this false sense of security (as well as a few jolts of John Barleycorn), had taken to publicly insulting the lawman.

During an argument with a fellow lowlife named Jeff Perkins and in the presence of Plummer, Cleveland accused Perkins of failing to repay a debt. When Plummer intervened on Perkins's behalf, Cleveland threatened Plummer. The sheriff drew his pistol, declared himself "tired of this," and shot Cleveland dead. Though he was eventually tried and acquitted of the crime (ruled self-defense), Plummer's reputation as a gunslinger was established. The incident also raised the eyebrows of the local newspaper. Local voters began reconsidering the sheriff's fitness for office.

Meanwhile, out on the trail, a new industry was emerging. As the wealth of gold was being transported out of the area via stagecoach, a band of robbers began taking notice. During a one-year period under Plummer's watch, more than a dozen stagecoaches were robbed, and one local was murdered by a highwayman.

Surprisingly, the behavior of the thieves made their identities common knowledge. By a strange coincidence they were typically broke one day and flush the next, their reappearance in town with pockets full of money seemingly corresponding with the timing of the robberies.

Their presence and behavior, coupled with the sheriff's lack of enthusiasm for putting the suspects behind bars, cast Plummer in a bad light. Was the sheriff involved in the robberies? He was a known acquaintance of many of the suspects. Locals also took note of the fact that his office was located in Chrisman's General Store, where miners sometimes discussed their travel plans. He was often out of town at about the same time that the stages left.

Eventually, in June of 1863, Deputy D. H. Dillingham began to suspect that his fellow deputies might be planning robberies. He confided his fear to other members of the community. Within days he was murdered by unknown assailants. But Plummer did not seem inclined to investigate the murder, raising further questions about his complicity.

Fueled by veiled accusations in the newspaper, public senti-ment shifted. People began thinking that their sheriff was a crook, even though his lifestyle had not changed and there was no hard evidence that he had been present at any of the robbery sites.

Among Plummer's most vocal critics was Thomas Dims-dale, who wrote a number of articles incriminating Plummer in the organization and management of the road agents. Dimsdale's accounts were certainly biased and prone to exaggeration, espe-cially since he had no hard evidence of the sheriff's guilt. They also were tainted by a Victorian moralism that couched events in terms of good versus evil. He described Plummer as "a very demon who committed outrages against the laws of God and man."

Dimsdale enjoyed scattered support in his criticism of the lawman. A former friend of Plummer, Nathaniel Langford, once said that he "lived in fear of his life," following a run-in with the sheriff. In the summer of 1863, during a short-lived friendship with Plummer, Langford was the president of the Union League, the equivalent of a modern business club. Plummer applied for membership, assuming that his friendship with Langford would help him along.

Due to the suspicion that Plummer was engaged in the stagecoach robberies, however, Langford personally rejected the application. When Plummer learned of Langford's action, the two engaged in a spirited discussion, at the end of which Plum-mer said, according to Langford, "You'll be sorry for this. I've always been your friend but from this time on I'm your enemy; and when I say this, I mean it in more ways than one."

The threat may have been the trigger the Vigilantes had been waiting for. Dimsdale and Langford, along with a number of other prominent politicians and businessmen, were among the founders of the Vigilantes. They were embarked on a three-year crusade to round up, try, convict, and execute anyone suspected of criminal activity in the territory. They followed their kangaroo trials by immediately hanging their victims.

When an outlaw named "Red" Yeager was arrested, he was coerced into implicating Plummer as a road agent. The sheriff was corralled on January 10, 1864, at which time he is said to have begged, argued, and pleaded his innocence. But one of the Vigilantes responded, "You are to be hanged. You cannot feel harder about it than I do, but I cannot help it if I would."

Convinced that he was headed for the hangman's noose, Plummer's last words were, "Now, men, as a last favor, let me beg that you will give me a good drop."

Interestingly, following the hangings of Plummer and his alleged cohorts, the robberies did not cease. In fact, by some accounts, intelligence among the thieves seemed to pass more quickly, there was an increase in organized criminal activity, and more robbers were involved.

From an historical standpoint, there is no agreement as to Plummer's guilt. Was he involved in the nefarious activities of the highway robbers? Or was he simply negligent or inept?

"We are not the first to conclude that there is no real evidence against Plummer," writer Dan Cushman is quoted in the biography *Hanging the Sheriff.* "The charges set forth would never have stood up in court. No actual proof exists that Plummer profited by a dollar from road agentry, or planned a robbery. His record was against him. He was destined for a gunman's grave or hangman's noose ever since his early days in California."

Since Plummer's death, the rumors and tales of his deeds have tended toward exaggeration, especially the rumor about how he might have had the foresight to bury a large portion of his ill-gotten gains before his death. How wealthy was he when he died? And where did the wealth go? One skeptical historian notes, "The only successful robbery was of the Magruder party, who left town with $14,000. When Langford wrote of the robbery the number has been inflated to $24,000. Merchants and suppliers came away from the gold camps with fortunes, not the miners or road agents."

Dimsdale is a particularly unreliable source. While acknowledging that Henry Plummer was never directly connected with the Magruder murder, he wrote, "There has always been a well-founded suspicion that he was the instigator of this most dreadful crime."

Historian Tom Lowe, assistant manager at Bannack State Park, also has a theory about Plummer's complicity in the events. In a letter dated April 27, 2006, he wrote:

> Whether he was actually the evil leader of a gang of
> bloodthirsty road agents, or an innocent victim in a

struggle for power and wealth during the Civil War is left for us to decide. We do know that Plummer killed four men in his brief life, always he claimed in self-defense. I personally think Plummer was dirty but I don't think he was guilty of everything he was accused of. He will forever be an enigma and a fascinating character in the history of Montana.

And what of the buried fortune? Tom Lowe continues:

There have been many stories told about a fantastic treasure of gold that Plummer and his gang hid before their deaths. The thought that a fortune in hidden gold awaits the lucky finder is the stuff that dreams are made of! People often ask me if I believe that millions of dollars in gold are really buried somewhere in the area. No one knows for sure but I don't believe any truly large cache of gold exists. Outlaws in general don't usually think very far ahead. Most of the bad boys would spend their ill-gotten gold as fast as they stole it. Whiskey, women, gambling, fast horses soon depleted their pokes. That didn't bother them though; they would just rob some other poor miner of his gold dust. I imagine there are some smaller caches of gold hidden in the area, and I have heard stories of the recovery of a few. It's great to fantasize about a golden hoard waiting for someone to discover its hidden location, but I won't waste my time looking for it.

An interesting side note, and as if to further disgrace the sheriff's memory, not long after his burial, Plummer's grave was vandalized. Two strangers passing through town dug up the corpse and detached the head from the body. The skull was then put on display at the Bank Exchange Saloon where it remained for several years, staring out at the citizens of Montana with a blank gaze and a toothy grin.

There's no doubt that Sheriff Henry Plummer was a short-tempered individual who knew how to handle a six-shooter. He was an acquaintance of men who lived on the wrong side of the law. But was he guilty of masterminding a series of highway robberies?

We will never know.

CHAPTER SEVEN

IS THERE A CONNECTION BETWEEN UFOS
AND CATTLE MUTILATIONS?

You might not think that the deaths of a few cows would, in the grand scheme of things, mean much to Montana's history. But you'd be wrong.

Back in 1975 a sheriff's office in northern Montana received a phone call that two cows had been mutilated on a ranch near Belt. This was the first in a series of alarms that would affect law enforcement officials in five counties—and conspiracy theorists for years. In addition to signaling the commencement of one of the greatest unsolved mysteries in Montana's history, the call also changed the life of Captain Keith Wolverton of the Cascade County Sheriff's Department. He would eventually devote three years of his life to trying to find an explanation for the mutilations.

When Wolverton arrived to investigate the scene of the mutilations, the deputy discovered that the cows' bag, teats, rectal area, and reproductive organs had been removed, apparently cut out by an instrument with a serrated edge.

Perplexed, he sent samples of the mutilations to a pathologist in Colorado. The report read, "This strip of skin had a long, straight cut edge with regular serrations. Hair in one area had knowingly been clipped. Changes on the skin edge resembled neither tooth marks of a predator, nor those of wire lacerations."

Coyotes may feed on a carcass, but they don't leave a serrated edge. Magpies and crows might peck at the eyes, the rectum, any soft flesh, but they don't tear it away. Add that evidence to the fact that reports of possible cattle mutilations had first occurred in August 1974, and the deputy was confronted with a major-league puzzle.

Then followed a growing number of reports of similarly mutilated cows, the circumstances of which made things even more puzzling. All of the animals had been dissected in the same manner, but there were never any tracks near the carcasses, even in fields of soft, loose dirt. In one puzzling instance, the left jaw of a cow was removed, as was its tongue and right eye. In that case a veterinarian discovered what appeared to be a needle mark in the left leg of the victim. Had the animal been anesthetized prior to death?

When another event occurred in Teton County, Sheriff Pete Howard asked Wolverton, who was quickly becoming the resident expert, to assist in evaluating what might have happened. A Shetland pony was found lying on its side with all of its male organs removed. A veterinarian also discovered two puncture wounds in the horse's throat. And the body contained no blood. The ground was dry and unstained. "A horse this size should have had sixty pints of blood in its body," the vet said.

In a similar investigation, when another mutilated cow was found without any blood, an animal pathologist in Colorado opined that removing all of a cow's blood is virtually impossible since, when one third is removed, the veins collapse. Then he added, "It could be accomplished by injecting a saline solution into the heart while the animal is alive." This would also speed the rate at which the heart would pump. "Saline is virtually impossible to detect in an autopsy."

Over the next two years, an increasing number of reports were filed. One cow in Cascade County was found in a newly plowed field three-quarters of a mile from the nearest road or fence. But there were no footprints in the area. Miles away, another rancher reported the disappearance of a newly born calf whose mother had been mutilated. The calf was never located.

With a drawer full of similar reports, Wolverton had his work cut out for him. Organs were being removed with surgical precision. The lack of footprints or tire tracks eliminated cultists. There were no animal tracks or any signs of predation on the bodies. But maybe the animals had been injected with a needle. Wolverton enlisted the help of both a veterinarian and a rancher who wanted to see an end to the mutilations.

The rancher offered Wolverton a calf. The vet injected it with a drug that doubled the calf's pulse rate. Another needle in the neck drained the blood. As a result, they confirmed that all of an animal's blood could be removed. After a transfusion and when the effect of the drug wore off twenty-five minutes later, the calf was back on its feet.

When winter arrived in 1975, law-enforcement officers in five counties were being overwhelmed with reports of mutilations, all of which were following the same pattern. And Montana wasn't the only state afflicted with the same mystery. Reports of mutilations in Colorado, Utah, Idaho, and Minnesota were also making news. In May 1976 Wolverton began contacting law enforcement authorities in other states. Two incidents in Minnesota caught his attention. In the first a cow had been mutilated in an area covered by 6 inches of snow. A 6-foot radius of snow surrounding the cow was melted, though there were no footprints or vehicle tracks in the area.

In a second episode a pig was mutilated. The owner of the pig reported, "Last evening, my yard light went out, and I assumed it was burnt out. Then, about twenty minutes later, it went back on." He discovered the mutilated pig the following morning.

Back in Montana, dispatchers had received reports of unidentified helicopters. But on the day that the sightings had occurred, the wind was blowing hard enough to ground the choppers at Malmstrom Air Force Base. When Wolverton explained to Air Force officials that the residents were becoming antsy, they agreed to broadcast the message that their choppers did not fly after dark. There were reports of as many as nine helicopters flying together near Lewistown. By November 1975 even the Air Force was on alert. Helicopters had been sighted near missile silos, after all, and this was in the middle of the Cold War. Early one evening, a farm family observed yet another helicopter hovering over a silo, "So low to the ground that at times it seemed to touch," one observer said. It was spotted heading north near Dutton. Thirty-eight minutes later, it was at a missile site near the Air Force base. During a hectic four hours, sightings were reported over an area spanning more than one hundred square miles. An hour after midnight, an officer sent to investigate saw a strobe light flying east but could not verify that it was a chopper. A sergeant at the missile site added, "The object did not sound like a conventional helicopter, and had only a single strobe light and no running lights."

The object had appeared on radar only to disappear within 5 miles of the base. An hour later, Air Force officers reported seeing an unidentified flying object near the same area as the one that had appeared the previous night. Ten minutes later, a sheriff received a report of a UFO that did not appear on the Malmstrom radar. When contacted by telephone, the man who had sighted the aircraft reported, "Clouds are beginning to cover the object." He described the craft as having been very close to the ground. And it appeared to have a yellow appearance that turned white as it climbed.

More sightings, often of two objects, were reported the following evening, this time by officers on patrol. None of the aircraft appeared on radar screens. All were in close proximity to missile sites.

By May 1975 the Cascade County Sheriff's Office had received reports of 130 sightings in a five-county area. Many were confirmed as being helicopters, though the Air Force denied involvement. One was attributed to the Montana Air National Guard, another to a Canadian helicopter on a training mission. The officers also were told of sightings in fields from which cows were missing.

Some of the aircraft were described as being saucer shaped or like "a giant pear." Or like "a two-story building with lights resembling windows." A common denominator was the speed at which they traveled. A farmer from Raynesford estimated the speed at which a UFO ascended at 5,400 miles per hour. When the sheriff suggested that the object might be a star or planet, the caller responded, "Then why can I see a mountain behind it?"

Two teenagers reported to Undersheriff Jerry Skelton a strange object hovering over their car, "It continued to stay above the car as we hurried home." When they arrived home, they alerted other family members who went outside to view the UFO. "[It] hovered over their house before leaving a short time later," according to Skelton's report.

The list of sightings in 1975 is almost endless—and endlessly confusing. In some cases UFO sightings occurred in the same area as cattle mutilations. In one case a rancher saw a UFO land in an area where he'd deposited a dead calf. A day after the sighting, the calf was nowhere to be found. But perhaps the most compelling sighting was confirmed by NORAD. An oblong-shaped UFO was tracked on radar for more than an hour, during which time its elevation ranged between 8,000 and 18,000 feet. Then the object disappeared from the screen but was still viewed by deputies who had been dispatched to track it. When radar contact was reestablished, the object was at 14,100 feet, moving slowly. When the UFO was last seen it had ascended from 14,750 feet to 44,500 feet at approximately 1,000 miles per hour before stopping suddenly, then disappearing.

But once you scratch under the surface, it turns out that Montana has a long history of UFO sightings, beginning back in the 1950s. On August 15, 1950, in Great Falls, Nick Mariana was climbing the grandstand of the Legion Ball Park at 11:25 in the morning. As he neared the top, he happened to look north toward the smokestack. A bright flash caught his eye. Two silvery objects were moving swiftly to the south. "My first thought was, get the camera, they're flying discs! Then I thought again, they must be planes in a bank, and I'll see their wings in just a minute. Then as they got closer and more distinct, I realized there were no wings. These were not banking planes, they were flying saucers!"

Yelling for his secretary, who was in a nearby parking lot, Mariana ran down the stairs to get his movie camera. He was able to shoot about twenty seconds of 16-millimeter film before the objects arced to the southeast behind the General Mills water tower. In all Mariana and his secretary observed the objects for about three-and-a-half minutes. His reel of grainy color footage was among the first to capture flying saucers on motion picture film.

Described as a "reliable, trustworthy and honest individual [who] is highly respected in the community," Mariana immediately reported the sighting to the local newspapers. He also sent the film to Chicago for processing and showed it to several civic groups around Great Falls in September and October. In addition he loaned the film to officials of the Air Force's Technical Intelligence Center (ATIC). The Air Force concluded that the objects were likely reflections off a couple of F-94 jets that were in the area.

"The Air Force, however, returned only *seven* feet of the *eight*-foot film," wrote historian John Axline in his master's thesis at Montana State University. The missing footage showed the objects rotating in unison as they hovered over the refinery before continuing their flight to the southwest.

The "Montana Film," as it later came to be known, represented one of several UFO sightings in the Great Falls area in the early 1950s. On August 29, two men in the Geyser area reported seeing a "silvery mass" with a long tail. Two Great Falls Air Force veterans later spotted "six amber colored objects flying over the city." In June 1951 the *Great Falls Tribune* reported that "Heinie Wilson saw twelve round white objects while on U.S. Highway 87," about 50 miles northeast of Great Falls. The newspaper jokingly stated, "You know, for a while things seemed like the good old days when the only objects that filled Montana skies were an occasional goose or a jet or two."

Given the UFO sightings occurring throughout the West— particularly Roswell, New Mexico—and the filming of other UFOs at Tremonton, Utah, the Air Force began reinvestigating many older UFO cases. In 1952 Air Force General and Project Blue Book Chief Edward J. Ruppelt reopened the Montana file. He interviewed Mariana, and Air Force specialists reanalyzed the film. They paid particular attention to the flight paths of the two F-94s that were in the vicinity when the sighting occurred. Ruppelt determined that the two jets had not been close to where the objects were sighted. Mariana stated that he and his secretary saw the jets land behind them *after* the UFOs had disappeared from view.

Ruppelt concluded, "We drew a blank on the Montana Movie—it was an unknown." In March 1956 Dr. Robert Baker, an astrophysicist employed by the Douglas Aircraft Company, published a report entitled, "Photogrammetric Analysis of the Montana Film Tracking Two UFOs." He said that the images on film "could not be explained by any presently known natural phenomenon. The linear path of the objects eliminated birds, as the reflections were too steady, and there was no evidence of flapping wings. They were not meteors because of the lack of a vapor trail, noise, or fragmentation. The logical explanation was reflection off the two F-94s." But Baker's report apparently eliminated that possibility. Indeed, Mariana and Baker seemed to believe that the objects had generated their own light.

Baker continued, "Throughout the sequence, the two images stand out from the sky background because of their intensity, sharpness, and constant relative orientation, one preceding the other in a smooth progression across the sky and behind the water tower." According to Baker's calculations, as the objects moved away from the camera, their velocity increased, reaching a speed that he estimated to be "faster than jets could fly at that time." The investigator concluded that "scientific analysis couldn't positively identify them with aircraft."

Popular interest in Mariana's film remained strong well into the 1960s. In 1966 the Air Force reopened its investigation into UFOs and organized the Condon Committee, which included twenty prominent scientists, including Baker. The task members were charged by the government to conduct an objective study into all sightings reported in recent years. When it published its findings, the "Montana Film" was one of fifty-nine cases reinvestigated by the committee. They concluded, "The Montana film remains unexplained . . . analysis indicated that the images on the film are difficult to reconcile with aircraft or other known phenomenon." Committee investigator David Saunders wrote in 1968 that the "Montana Film" was "the one sighting of all time that did more than any other single case to convince me that there *is* something to the UFO problem."

But why did the Air Force keep three seconds of the original footage?

"I don't have an answer or even a theory," historian Jon Axline says. "In the case of the Montana Film, it involves the film itself. When Nick Mariana turned the film over to ATIC in October 1950, the air force initially claimed that the images on the film were 'too dark to distinguish any recognizable objects.' The film belies that claim in that it clearly shows two objects moving through the sky.

"My main contention is that the film doesn't represent the entire footage shot by Mariana. In 1967, Condon Committee investigator Roy Craig interviewed two men in Great Falls who saw the film before it was sent to ATIC. John Wuertner, Mariana's attorney, saw the entire film. 'The main part that I recall that didn't come back,' he said, 'was when it was right overhead. Now it started in the east and as it arose on the horizon then there was a part cut out and all we have left was the part disappearing over the west.'"

An acquaintance of Mariana's, Tony Dalich, said, "Maybe two or three feet of the film was missing." He remembered "two objects, definitely spinning, shaped like a wafer of peppermint candy." Both men agreed that the missing footage showed the objects in better detail than what is present on the existing film. The Air Force trimmed additional frames of the film sometime between 1952 and 1976.

"In the face of the evidence," says Axline, "my historian's mind tends to lean towards Mariana's belief that they were flying saucers. But one can never be sure and it will likely remain one of Montana's greatest mysteries."

All was quiet on the Montana front for nearly a quarter of a century. Then in 2001, eight cow killings were reported in the vicinity of Dupuyer. All of the carcasses bore a striking resemblance to the mutilations of the 1970s.

For ranchers and law enforcement officials along the remote Rocky Mountain Front, it was, as Yogi Berra would have said, "Déjà vu all over again." Pete Howard, the Choteau County justice of the peace, said, "We had a bunch of them. I've lived in this county all my life and worked on ranches and seen plenty of dead animals, but never did I see an animal with its face mask removed like that."

Cattle rancher Brian Schweitzer, who was later elected governor of Montana, found a cow killed in the same manner. "The brand inspector said it was lightning, but there was no lightning that night," Schweitzer said. "And it very much looked like those incisions were done with instruments. But I said fine, there's a lot of things I can't explain."

Law enforcement officials and ranchers were split over the cause of death, some attributing it to a lightning strike, a wolf kill, cultists, or the re-arrival of the Little Green Men. "This publicity is awful," said Leland P. Cade, former editor of the *Montana-Farmer Stockman.* "City people don't know what's going on, and they envision crazy people doing weird things to animals in the night. The cattle were probably killed by predators. Now we have a brand-new crop of ignorant people who don't know what goes on on the range."

But Dan Campbell, who was raised on an area ranch, said, "People who dismiss the deaths are not looking hard enough. No vehicle tracks or footprints have been found around the animals. Cuts made to remove the tissue are very clean. There are smooth edges on those cuts. They are not bite marks."

Four years later, sitting over a cup of coffee in Choteau, Campbell still dismissed the predator explanation. Previously with the sheriff's department, he later became an investigator for the Department of Livestock. During that time, he saw "carcasses of cattle up in the trees on a ranch. They didn't climb up there. And we found dead cattle on the ground that had clearly been dropped from some type of aircraft because there was a deep impression on the ground." He also noted that the cow's skin "had a green glow to it." He attributes the fact that they were not eaten by coyotes or other critters to the presence "of some type of chemical."

Credible or not, there is at least one scientific explanation to the events of the 1970s and 2001. In the words of the "Summary Report on a Wave of UFO/Helicopters and Animal Mutilations in Cascade County, Montana, 1974–1977," published by the National Institute for Discovery Science (NIDS), Las Vegas, in 2002, the answer lies in a massive cover-up of infections that can be transmitted to humans by sick cows. The report states, "Although animal mutilation research has been immersed in a miasma of wild speculation, false claims, and unscientific methodology, there is considerable evidence that the phenomenon is real."

The two central and unanswered questions that have dogged research into this phenomenon are (a) Who? and (b) Why?

The conclusion of the report, taken at face value, is quite alarming. The authors propose that there is a link between the mutilations and the contamination of herds of cattle by a class of disease-causing agents known as prions—believed to be the cause of "mad cow" disease.

Further, the NIDS report hypothesizes that patterns of animal mutilations are consistent with a covert infectious disease–monitoring operation. Montana was not alone when it experienced the mutilations and sightings of strange aircraft. In addition to the scores of cases in northeastern Colorado, hundreds of other animal mutilation reports were investigated by local law enforcement in fifteen states, from South Dakota and Montana to New Mexico and Texas. Many anecdotal reports have claimed the presence of black or unmarked helicopters in the area of animal mutilations.

But why leave the carcasses?

NIDS says, "One of the most quoted hypotheses involves a government operation to monitor radiation or biological warfare testing. But the question, 'Why leave the body?' has never been adequately answered. The government can just as easily test their own herds, the counter-argument goes, or obtain carcasses from a slaughterhouse. For this and many other reasons, the evidence points away from the government as perpetrators of animal mutilations."

The report classifies the mutilations and abandonment of the bodies as "a brutal warning." It suggests that attention is being deliberately focused on the mutilated animals. "Further, we suggest the human food chain is compromised, probably with a prion-associated infectious agent that still remains mostly undetected."

In an even bolder statement, NIDS prophesies, "Mutilations will be followed, years or even decades later, by a TSE [mad cow] outbreak." And that "a rather large outbreak of CWD/TSE will occur in the area around Great Falls, Montana, in the next several years."

We have a tempest in a teapot. Given the Montana Film and the numerous UFO sightings, it is difficult to completely discount the presence, at one time or another, of UFOs in the skies above Montana. Perhaps space travelers were cruising the galaxy and decided to pay a visit to our planet? Regardless of their origin, the cattle mutilations are a fact that no one seems to be able to explain. The government hasn't stepped forward to confess, and twenty-five years of investigation has yet to produce a reliable conclusion.

We are stuck, it would seem, with what legitimately qualifies as a Montana mystery.

CHAPTER EIGHT

IF BIGFOOT EXISTS, HE NEEDS A SHOWER . . .

As if the Montana state police and sheriffs in five counties didn't have enough on their plate with the epidemic of cattle mutilations in 1975 and 1976, they were also being treated to an outbreak of Bigfoot sightings.

If you have not personally crossed paths with a Bigfoot, here's what you can expect to see, based on a random sampling of comments. He (or she) is a furry, gorilla type creature approximately 8 feet tall with dark eyes and the musculature of Arnold Schwarzenegger. The features are a combination of human and ape, with a wide nose, slanted forehead and flat, forward-sloping eyebrows. The head has a pronounced cone-shaped top. The neck is short, and the chin juts outward. The close-cropped ears are small and covered by hair. The skin on the face, hands, and feet is dark and leathery. The arms are long with the hands falling below the knees. In rare instances, both juveniles and adults have been seen walking on all fours.

The Bigfoot Field Researchers Organization (BFRO), a pioneer in Bigfoot study, lists 1,989 sightings dating back to the 1800s. Washington apparently holds the record for the most sightings in the United States, with 296 documented cases. Other contenders are California, 281; Ohio, 158; and Oregon and Texas, with 149 and 106, respectively.

Though the number of sightings in Montana pales by comparison with other states, there is an abundance of evidence that suggests the presence of these shy creatures in the Treasure State. If you run into him in the woods, however, and he doesn't respond to "Bigfoot," you might try calling him, "Bad Indian," "Mountain Devil," "Omaha Bushman," "Sasquatch," "Yeren," or "Yeti." Scientists have sometimes referred to him as *Gigantopithecus blacki,* an extinct primate that lived in Asia 300,000 years ago. Maybe he wandered to North America over a frozen Bering Strait, though Bigfoot literature is filled with theories regarding his origins. Because nighttime sightings are more frequent than daytime sightings, it's supposed that the creature is nocturnal. When a Bigfoot is encountered at close range, some witnesses report smelling a rank odor of rotting flesh, ammonia, or sulfur. The reports of the odor are so frequently connected to Florida sightings that locals refer to the critters as "Skunk Apes."

The first of Montana's sightings was reported on December 26, 1975, when a pair of high school students described to sheriff's deputies near Vaughn how their horses had been acting strangely that afternoon. When the girls ventured out to the corral to determine the cause of the uproar, they had seen a "strange creature two hundred yards from the house." One of the two kids grabbed a rifle—not to shoot the creature but to use the telescopic sight—and saw "a dark and awful face that did not look human."

When she fired the rifle into the air, the creature fell to the ground and began crawling toward a thicket of trees. The girls then observed several other, similarly grotesque creatures reaching from the thicket to assist their compatriot. After recounting their tale to deputies, both girls took polygraph tests. They seemed to be telling the truth.

Then one of their parents added to the mystery. He'd apparently been awakened the night before by a sound "like a human dying an agonizing death." People who see Bigfoot commonly report bloodcurdling screams associated with the sightings. About one month later, deputies were told by a man living miles away that he had heard a similar sound. And again, a few weeks later, a lady living in Babb had a comparable report.

Two months later, boys ages twelve and thirteen were near the Missouri River when one saw a hairy arm extending from the brush. The second boy saw a very tall creature covered with blackish brown hair and with eyes that glowed whitish yellow. When the incident was reported to Cascade County law enforcement officer, Keith Wolverton, both lads also passed the polygraph test.

Near Great Falls in March 1976, a fifteen-year-old boy reported seeing a hairy creature that he described as, "a

ILLUSTRATIONS BY RICK C. SPEARS

While most descriptions of Bigfoot tend to be strikingly similar, there is some variation, as portrayed here by artist Rick C. Spears.

Sasquatch-like thing" standing on Dempsey Road. Once again, the sheriff said, "The boy passed a polygraph test, no problem."

One of the most credible Bigfoot sightings in Montana occurred on April 4, 1976, when the critters began making themselves openly conspicuous. A sixteen-year-old boy living near Helena told deputies that he was awake at 5:00 A.M. standing at a second story window overlooking a pasture, when he saw "a tall, hairy creature" walking toward the house. He described the creature as being covered entirely with long black or brown hair. He said the nose looked pushed in, and he didn't notice any ears. He estimated its height at 8 feet.

Then the creature was joined by an acquaintance, and both began walking toward the house. When they saw the lad at the window, they scampered away. Naturally the lad was terrified, but later in the day he and a sister found tracks of the creature and made a plaster cast. Deputies measured the footprint as being 17 inches long and 7 inches wide and having three toes.

Upon further investigation the deputies learned from the lad's father that, a week earlier, he had heard strange noises outside. While inspecting the area around the house, he had found large footprints in the snow. After the interview, both deputies agreed that the boy did see what he reported.

Around the same time two loggers traveling near Arlee saw something moving in a clearing above the road. It was tall enough to stand above some young pines, making it about 8 feet tall. It was covered with two-toned, rust-colored hair on its shoulders and chest and black hair on its legs. "We went around a corner where we couldn't see it anymore, and when we did it screamed a very loud, high pitched scream," they reported.

In March 2004 two travelers in western Montana saw another hairy creature. It was a sunny Sunday afternoon, and a mother was driving in the company of her daughter's fifteen-year-old boyfriend along the highway above the Clark Fork River, en route to St. Regis where they would be picking up the daughter. As they crossed the river, the mother "noticed the ice was breaking up from around the edges and floating downstream. As we started over the bridge that spans the river I looked to my left, as I always do. There is a sand bar that reaches out into the river on the west side and near the tip I saw a very tall, eight to ten feet, hairy being and a much smaller one. It looked to be right at or just taller then the knee of the larger one.

"The larger one was standing about five to six feet behind the small one with its arms outstretched and taking a step forward. The small one looked as if it was curious about the chunks of ice that were near the water's edge, as it was leaning forward looking down. The tall one had long reddish brown hair. I remember seeing it flow from the upper arm area, and the hair on its head and shoulders was also long.

"When I saw them I said to my daughter's boyfriend, 'Look at that!' He said, 'Whoa!' then we were over the bridge. We didn't turn around, I think we were stunned and didn't quite believe what we had just seen, maybe a bit scared too?"

There was no sign of the Bigfoot when they recrossed the river on the return trip, and neither she nor her passenger mentioned the sighting. "I'd been trying to convince myself I didn't really see what I saw," she recalled.

"Then, one night at dinner, I told my family what I had

seen. My daughter's boyfriend happened to be there for dinner and said, 'I remember that, I was there with you!'"

Did she see a mother Bigfoot and her young child?

"I got the feeling in that brief moment that she was showing her young one something new, allowing him or her to explore. Perhaps her baby had gone too close to the river, and she was reaching out as if to say, 'That's far enough!' as I've done with my own children."

The following July, in the same vicinity, a witness who chooses to remain anonymous reported to The Bigfoot Field Researchers Organization, a group founded in 1995, a sighting at the edge of her backyard on the Flathead Indian Reservation near Evaro. Dogs were barking, and when she ventured outside, she saw movement in the trees. "I watched to see what caught my eye, and then I saw the creature. It was behind the tree looking out from behind it. Its head was large, and it had a definite brow, so I thought I was seeing an orangutan." She described its eyes as haunting.

To confirm what she thought she saw, she went into her house and watched through the window to make sure it wasn't a trick of shadow. "Then the creature moved in front of the tree, staying hunched over but watching me in the window." The creature eventually departed. "But when my husband came home we went out to the tree, and all of the knapweed was completely trampled down around the tree."

Fast-forward to January 2006, when Bruce Schildt and his two sons notified the Blackfeet Fish and Wildlife Department of tracks found on the reservation. By Schildt's reckoning the tracks were about 18 inches long and 10 inches wide, and attached to legs that produced a 39-inch stride. "There were thirty or forty tracks," said Schildt, including one very clear print.

The tracks were discovered by the boys during a hike. "The footprints looked like barefoot human footprints, but they were about three times as big," said Schildt. "They were frozen in the mud up there."

Professor Jeffrey Meldrum of Idaho State University has staked his professional reputation—and perhaps his job—on the existence of Bigfoot. A tenured member of the faculty who teaches anatomy, the professor is convinced of the reality of Bigfoot based on an incident that occurred ten years ago. While scouring the woods in eastern Washington he came upon a 15-inch footprint, which he initially dismissed as being a hoax. But then he noticed locked joints in the impression and a narrow arch; features that he felt could belong only to a Bigfoot. "That's what set the hook," he said. "I was resolved it was a question I'd get to the bottom of."

With a steady paycheck, and a $30,000 donation from another true believer, he now spends his spare time exploring the woods in search of the reclusive critter.

Back on the home front, however, things are not so cheery.

Idaho State Uuniversity Professor of Physics Martin Hackworth dismisses Meldrum's work as "a joke," while Professor D. P. Wells wonders aloud if Meldrum, "also will research Santa

Claus." And Dean of Arts and Sciences John Kijinski admits, "There have been grumblings about Meldrum's tenure, but no formal request for a review has been forthcoming."

Short of catching a glimpse of Bigfoot ourselves, however, the rest of us are left to wonder, is he real or imagined, is he Yeti or *Gigantopithecus blacki?* Or maybe pranksters have been dressing up in Halloween costumes. But it is hard to dismiss the number of independent, unrelated sightings reported over the years, most of them by individuals who don't seem to care for fame or fortune.

One sure fact remains, however: If Bigfoot does exist in Montana, he needs a shower.

CHAPTER NINE

WHO NAMED THE CRAZY MOUNTAINS?

If measured by the height and number of spectacular peaks, not to mention downright beauty, the Crazy Mountains near Big Timber may be the most underrated mountain range in the Rockies. Often referred to as the Crazies, they have a tendency to collect mysteries.

Located between the Musselshell and Yellowstone Rivers, the range rises more than 6,000 feet above the plains to the east. Running for 50 miles north to south and 15 miles east to west, they dominate their surroundings, plainly visible for miles from Interstate 90, Highway 89, and Highway 287.

The mountains' first human inhabitants were Stone Age hunters. An archaeological dig on the west side of the mountains unearthed a site that produced tools thought to have been used more than 11,500 years ago. The next known occupants of the area were the Shoshone Indians, who set up camp about 1,000 years ago. The Shoshone weren't very warlike so when the Crow and Blackfeet tribes, and later, white men, arrived on the scene, the Shoshone packed up and departed.

Since Lewis and Clark left their footprints in nearly every other zip code in Montana, it only makes sense that they would have passed through this area, though these mountains remain one of the few landmarks they did not name. While following the Yellowstone River where it runs near the foothills of the mountains, William Clark camped at the confluence of the Yellowstone and Shields Rivers on July 15, 1806. The following night he and his party slept at "Rivers Across" near Big Timber, the spot where Otter Creek and the Boulder River flow into the Yellowstone.

So, who is responsible for naming these spectacular peaks?

Archaeologist Larry Lahren tells us, "The Crow Indians called them the Mad Mountains because of their steepness, rugged beauty, and haunting winds." Other Crow names for peaks in the Crazies are Awahawapiia (Rugged Mountains), Bird Home Mountains, Mean Mountains, and Blue Bird Mountains. They referred to the tallest peak as Ahwahhawa Peak, which means Mad Mountain. The Crows believed the mountains to be inhabited by angry and vicious spirits.

It might also not be a coincidence that the flora and fauna of the area includes loco weed, a toxic plant that can sicken livestock if they eat it, turning them confused and disoriented.

Even the geology of the mountains adds to the mystery of the name. Rocks in the southern part of the mountains tend to be composed of sodic plagioclase, biotite, hornblende, and augite,

One of southern Montana's most striking landmarks, the Crazy Mountains are visible for miles from every direction.

while in the northern part of the range they are augite, olivine, biotite, alkali feldspar, and sodalite. Geologists are still trying to solve the mystery of how two entirely different rock types came to form the same mountain range.

Yet another theory is that the mountains were named after a member of the Crow Tribe. In this version, a woman who went mad moved to the mountains and sought refuge amidst the peaks. They became the "Crazy Woman Mountains." Legend has it that members of the tribe became her caregivers. Similarly, in his novel *Mountain Man,* Vardis Fisher penned a character named Sam Minard, an intellectually minded loner. His character was patterned after the real-life mountain man John "Liver Eating" Johnson. In Fisher's tale, during one of his hunting excursions around the Yellowstone River, Minard came upon a tragic scene. While in her cabin cooking dinner, a woman named Kate Bowden had heard the screams of her children. Rushing outside, she discovered that her husband and two sons had been brutally murdered by Indians and the attackers were raping her daughter.

Fisher describes Bowden turning upon the attackers. "She moved with such devastating speed and her blows were so unerring that four warriors fell before any of them realized that an avenger was upon them." When the carnage was over, "Kate Bowden stood, shuddering with rage and tremors and lunacy, her dead children and four dead Indians around her."

Sam Minard comes upon Bowden and, ever the good Samaritan, finds a shovel in her camp and is about to begin digging graves, when "she came running toward him, gesturing, like a mute. He followed her and she climbed to a tableland that was high enough to overlook the river and its bottom. . . . She took the shovel and marked off three spots. Then, convulsed, it seemed to Sam, by frustration or anguish, she fell to her knees."

In the years to come, and on the many occasions when he was near the Yellowstone, Minard checked on Kate's condition. They never spoke, and she rarely acknowledged his presence as her mind drifted farther from reality. He usually killed a deer or two for her larder and provisioned her cupboard at the beginning of every winter.

On his last visit he toted a sack of wildflowers for her spring garden. "[He] came to the hill where he had always paused to look at the shack and the garden and cried aloud 'My God!' and some part of him died. He saw the second cairn of stones, standing close by the one he had built, and he knew that Kate was dead."

Did Vardis Fisher somehow unveil the true history behind the name of the mountain range? Or did the name arise from the account of the Crow Indians?

Whatever the source, Spike Van Cleve probably got it right when he wrote in *Forty Years' Gatherin's,* "It's a good country. Where a man can sit in his saddle and see all across to the west stretch the Crazies, and swinging in the stirrups, a man has to throw back his head to follow their abrupt shoulders up to the white crests of the peaks."

That pretty much sums it up.

CHAPTER TEN

MEET FLESSIE, THE MONSTER OF FLATHEAD LAKE

Everybody knows about Nessie, the famed monster of Loch Ness, a deep lake in Scotland. Nessie was first sighted by a man named Mackenzie in October 1871. The creature moved slowly at first and then picked up speed. It looked like a log, then an upturned boat. Fourteen years later, Roderick Matheson reported another sighting. "The biggest thing I ever saw in my life, with a neck like a horse with a mane." More recently, on June 17, 1998, Adam and Mark Sutherland, Peter Gillies, and Peter Rhind saw a creature emerge, then submerge again. "It was a large object with a long tail," they reported.

Despite Nessie's fame, Scotland does not have a corner on the monster market. In fact, sightings of unusual swimming creatures have been reported from all corners of the globe. It turns out that Montana's Flathead Lake is ideal habitat for an underwater monster. The largest freshwater lake west of the Mississippi, it's 28 miles long, 15 miles wide, has 185 miles of shoreline, and, at least in spots, is hundreds of feet deep.

Montana Historical Society, Helena

The largest natural lake in Montana, Flathead Lake is rumored to hide its very own Loch Ness monster.

The first sighting of a creature in the lake was reported in 1889, when passengers on the steamer *US Grant* were amazed to see a "whalelike monster" approaching the boat. One passenger, apparently fearing for his life, fired rifle shots at the creature. Since then, the frequency of monster sightings has increased, with more than ninety having been reported before the year 2000. Taking the words "Flathead" and "Nessie," the creature has been dubbed "Flessie" by the locals.

Considering the history of the region, it makes sense that a prehistoric-type critter might inhabit the lake. About 12,000 years ago, the valleys of western Montana lay under a lake nearly 2,000 feet deep, formed when an ice sheet dammed what is now the Clark Fork River. This interior ocean was as big as Lake Erie and Lake Ontario combined. The waters continued to rise until the pressure against the ice dam became too much. When the dam failed, it produced a flood that raged west across Idaho, Oregon, and Washington. The deluge ran between 30 and 50miles per hour, with a force equal to sixty Amazon Rivers. The thundering waves picked up boulders the size of buses and deposited them 500 miles away.

Parts of central and eastern Montana were also once underwater and are known to have been home to herds of dinosaurs and other prehistoric animals.

Could Flessie be a prehistoric holdover? Maybe after the ice dam burst, Flessie got stuck in the newly created Flathead Lake. Even Laney Hanzel, who was a Fish, Wildlife, and Parks biologist

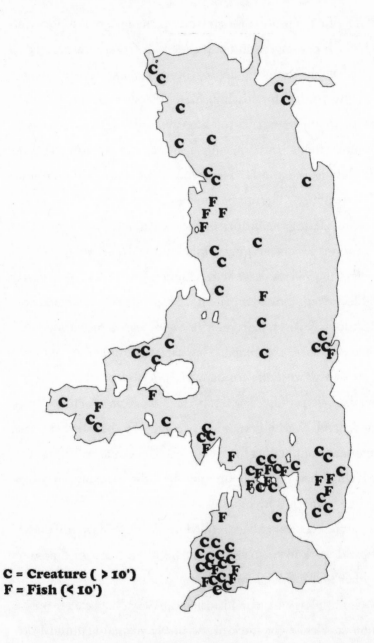

C = Creature (> 10')
F = Fish (< 10')

FLATHEAD LAKE CREATURE FIGURE COURTESY OF LANEY HANZEL

Eighty-one unusual sightings on Flathead Lake, 1889–1994

on Flathead Lake for more than thirty years, does not dismiss the possibility. "It is scientifically possible that there is something in the lake," he said.

Those fortunate enough to have seen Flessie in action have described the monster as being between 8 and 20 feet long, with gray to black coloring, and having three or more humps on its back. When moving on the surface, the monster creates a wake 8 to 12 inches tall, about the same as a powerboat.

While taking samplings of life in the lake, Hanzel experienced "several occurrences of my net being damaged. It had big holes in it that we can't explain."

Of the reported sightings, he said, "I think they are as real as people say they are. I've interviewed people and, without asking any questions, just listened to their descriptions, and they are all remarkably similar in describing the behavior and appearance of the creature. Many of them occurred during the evening hours, and were preceded by the sighting of a school of fish flying across the surface."

Hanzel has tallied eighty-one different accounts, most of them describing an eel-like monster "with humps and smooth skin. . . . I don't know what the thing is. It could be something from prehistoric ages."

In 2005 Paul Fugleberg of Polson, former publisher of the *Lake County Leader* and author of a booklet entitled *Montana Nessie of Flathead Lake,* has chronicled every sighting of the monster since 1889. Many of the sightings occurred near the Narrows on the south end of the lake, near Polson, and around Wild Horse Island. In August 1947, as Fugleberg describes it, a dozen people observed a huge fish estimated to be 20 feet long, brown, shaped like a fish. Later that same month, other witnesses "observed a large fish estimated to be about 20 feet long, and very fast, that remained in the area for a while before disappearing." Multiple sightings have been reported annually, the only exception being 2004.

Most accounts are very believable and include sightings by two or more witnesses. For example, in March 1953, fifteen mill workers watched "a big fish swimming about 200 yards from the Polson waterfront." Two years later, when Mr. and Mrs. Neil DeGolier thought they saw an overturned boat on Skidoo Bay, "They could see it was a huge fish that they watched roll on the lake surface for several minutes."

The spring and summer of 1963 were good years for Flessie sightings, as several families, and two high-school teachers, in separate sightings, saw "a dark gray object with three humps" and "a seven-foot-long fish cavort playfully in the Narrows."

Two of the most detailed accounts come from a Major George Cote in 1985 and 1987. His first sighting was in Yellow Bay. "We saw a large object surfacing and diving off the north point. We approached the thing slowly. As we got close, we could see it was chasing squawfish in the shallows. At one point it raised its head high and appeared to be looking at us.

"When we got to within 60 meters of it, we realized that it

was nothing we'd ever seen. The thing was big: as long as a telephone pole and twice as large in diameter. The skin was smooth and coal black; it had the perfect head of a serpent. There were four to six humps sticking out of the water. It moved away from us slowly, then took off like a streak."

The second sighting occurred on July 1, 1987. Major Cote said, "I've caught bluefin tuna over 1,000 pounds. I've seen sturgeon. I've been out on Flathead Lake over 300 times in the last 25 years, and I know what a submerged log looks like. I know what I saw. There's no doubt in my mind that it was a huge creature."

Most recently, an August 2005 report in the *Bigfork Eagle* recounted the experience of Polson attorney Jim Manley and wife, Julia. The couple was taking a snooze aboard a boat anchored in Big Arm bay early one evening. "We began hearing rhythmic splashing," Julia says. "Then we saw a mysterious oddity splashing for several minutes in Big Arm Bay. It was loud. After about three splashes we both opened our eyes and looked out on the water and then at each other to see whether we were seeing the same thing."

"It had a serpentine look," Jim added, "with several humps visible above the water. It moved slowly away from shore toward Wild Horse Island." Both agreed that "it wasn't a log, and it was moving against the current. The wind was a little breezy, and the lake was mostly calm except for the splashing of the dark-colored thing."

"It was something very large," Julia said.

They watched it for two to three minutes and judged it to be about 25 feet long. It was 75 to 100 yards away. A few feet separated the rounded humps as they rose nearly 2 feet out of the water. "It wasn't an optical illusion," Jim said. "The part above surface looked about as long as our boat. What really struck us was how loud the splashing was. It was regular, like waves breaking on a beach."

On the same day that the Manleys reported the incident, Hanzel was taking the report of a second sighting. Three-year-old Andrew Johnson had a real life encounter with Flessie, or says he did.

While Andrew's mom, Cindy, and Cindy's sister were preparing for a boat trip on the lake, Andrew headed for the water on his own. Walking down to the dock, he took an unplanned dip into the lake. His mother flew into a panic. The youngster didn't know how to swim, and he was literally in over his head.

But within seconds, Andrew had been hoisted back onto the dock by an unknown and unseen rescuer. In his words, "the Flathead monster lifted me up with his tail."

A lad of few words, he added, "She has a baby, too."

So as far as Andrew is concerned, not only is Flessie real but it has started a family, too.

CHAPTER ELEVEN

THERE ARE GHOSTS IN THE BUTTE ARCHIVES, AREN'T THERE?

When the respected likes of Doctor Ellen Baumler, interpretive historian at the Montana Historical Society and author of *Spirit Tailings;* Tom Lowe, assistant manager of Bannack State Park; and Shirley Smith, a Fromberg business owner, all give independent descriptions of paranormal spirits in Montana, it's perhaps time to give the topic a little attention.

First though, a primer: According to Eric and Kris Bratlien of Missoula, father and son founders of Tortured Souls Investigations (TSI)—an organization devoted to checking out reports of hauntings and, when possible, capturing the spirits on film— ghosts come in several flavors. "There are *residuals,*" Kris said. "They are like a recording that repeats itself. Footsteps, voices, sounds, and even apparitions, for instance." This type of haunting typically won't interact with its surroundings and is unaware of people witnessing it.

"A *poltergeist,*" Eric added, "is misunderstood as being a

TORTURED SOULS INVESTIGATIONS OF MISSOULA, MONTANA

According to Eric and Kris Bratlein, the former territorial prison at Deer Lodge—as evidenced by these vaporous apparitions—holds rich potential for those wishing to investigate paranormal activity.

demonic presence. In fact, *poltergeist* translates from German to *noisy ghost.* A poltergeist likes to play jokes and tricks on people, typically opening and slamming doors, or dousing lights."

Then there are *anomalies,* occurrences that are captured on film. According to Eric, these may be ectoplasm, ectomist, vapor, or a ghostly mist. Ecto has apparently been caught on both video and still cameras, most often at cemeteries, battlefields, and historical sites. Then there are *orbs.* "The most photographed anomalies captured on film. They show up as transparent or translucent balls of light hovering above the ground. They are believed to be the soul or spirit of those that have passed on from this life. We believe orbs are not ghosts but energy associated with paranormal energy."

Finally, there are *shadow ghosts,* which typically have the appearance of ectomist, but with form. "They are usually sneaky and evasive," Eric said. "When they are spotted it's usually out of the corner of your eye, or as they are darting through a wall, or in a mirror."

Ellen Crain is manager of the Butte-Silver Bow Archives. "I am not a big believer in ghosts and the paranormal," she confessed, "and quite frankly the less I know about the subject the better off I am. But this is my story and I am sticking to it.

"In the past ten years of working in and taking care of the Old Fire Hall on Quartz Street, where the archives are located, I have finally succumbed to the fact that the living are sharing space with someone. Every time I've thought that I've imagined the sound of water running or the voices of men at a card table, I have someone else who says, 'Did you hear that?' I have heard bells ringing and water gushing to the point I was concerned for my mental health, when to my gratitude a very sane, well-dressed individual would say, 'My, this is a very uncomfortable place. The water runs all the time and you are not answering the doorbell.'

"The most alarming thing that has ever happened to me, however, was during the summer of 1995. I came to work and stopped to count the cobblestones lining the garden when I turned and looked at the building and in the coffee room window was a woman standing there wiping her hands on a dishtowel. She had on an apron. So I sat down and had a cigarette." Not because she was postponing another day at the office; she was terrified. At the time she decided not to discuss the event with coworkers.

"Several years after this incident, Mike Burns was rummaging around in the Photo Archives at the World Museum of Mining and found some great photographs of the Fire Station taken around 1913. In one of the photographs, the fire chief is jumping out of the window onto a net to test it out, and in the window is the image of a woman drying her hands on a dishtowel. This is the same image I saw in the window two summers previously."

For their part Eric and Kris Bratlien formed TSI to explore accounts just like Ellen Crain's. Part of what they do is organize formal expeditions, hoping to demonstrate to their clientele instances of paranormal activity. A recent tour of the former state prison in Deer Lodge—a site with a history of both bloody violence and ghostly apparitions—was conducted during the late night and early morning of April 15 and 16, the forty-seventh anniversary of an uprising by inmates. That incident had resulted in the murder of the associate warden and, ultimately, the murder-suicide of two criminals.

On a tour of the prison with the Bratliens and the prison's business manager, Julia Smith, it didn't take long to become enveloped in the mystery of the prison. "Visitors to the prison often produce unsolicited comments about unusual experiences. One lady on a tour came out of the solitary confinement cell, took me aside, and asked if someone had died in that cell. She said that it had the feeling of death." (For the record, no known death occurred in that space.) "And a photographer who was on his own left earlier than he had planned after telling me that the solitary confinement cell was 'filled with evil.'"

The prison's history isn't one of the brightest spots in Montana lore. When the territory's bad apples became too great a nuisance, the legislature requested funds from the federal government in 1866 for the purpose of constructing a prison. While Congress agreed that the territory needed a prison, the funds they allocated for the construction were inadequate.

It wasn't until July 2, 1871, that the prison was finally finished. On that day Samuel Hughes became Deer Lodge inmate number one. His sentence for assault with intent to kill was nineteen years, but because the prison had only fourteen cells, he was pardoned by the governor and released six months later. Like a game of dominoes, every time a new inmate arrived a current resident was pardoned, even though the convict being released might have been more dangerous than his replacement.

As the state's population increased, it enjoyed a corresponding increase in the crime rate. Overcrowding at the prison became a chronic problem. It would be a century before the original facility was abandoned in favor of a replacement facility 5 miles west of town.

Before its closing, though, two more hoodlums and a new warden would add their stamp to the facility's unfortunate history. When Jerry Myles and Lee Smart, two career criminals, and Warden Floyd Powell arrived in 1958, discipline was in a shambles. Powell wrote that the use of pills and narcotics was rampant. He described gambling, payoffs, and "other nefarious activity."

Before taking residence in Deer Lodge's old prison, Jerry Myles's forte had been burglary. He had been in and out of various prisons since the age of ten. Acclimating to Deer Lodge, he quickly became a "con boss," a king of the hill, and a homosexual predator. With the arrival of Powell and the new deputy warden, Theodore Rothe, in 1958, Myles was often consigned to solitary confinement, where he spent many lonely hours plotting revenge.

Myles's coconspirator, Lee Smart, was already a convicted killer and was willing to kill again in order to escape confinement. By the afternoon of April 15, 1959, a Thursday, the duo had recruited several convicts to stage an uprising, which they hoped would result in their freedom.

In short order, they overcame the guards in their cellblock by dousing them with flammable naptha stolen from the garment shop. They then commandeered the kitchen, as well as the second cellblock, and strolled casually to the administration building. There they overpowered guards and took the entire staff hostage. Unaware of the revolt, Deputy Warden Rothe was sitting behind his desk when Myles and Smart arrived, taking him by surprise. Smart killed Rothe with a rifle shot through the heart.

Warden Powell, who was outside the prison walls at the time of the uprising, began negotiating the release of twenty-one hostages. After a thirty-six-hour standoff, on Friday evening the warden decided that the time had come to retake his facility. With assistance from the National Guard, he led a successful assault on the main gate. After the hostages were freed, his focus shifted to Myles, Smart, and three other convicts who had taken refuge in the northwest guard tower. At Powell's urging the three tagalongs surrendered, leaving Myles and Smart on their own.

The two ringleaders made their decision quickly. When the guard stormed the tower, Smart shot Myles, then committed suicide.

It was into this history that we interjected ourselves for the anniversary tour. Shortly after our arrival, Kris began recounting events from the previous evening's walk-through. One young lady who had been alone in the prison's darkened theater felt her hair being pulled from behind. In another part of the prison, she had also described an "eerie feeling." And during the wee hours after the visitors left, TSI's infrared recorders filmed the presence of unexplainable patterns of light in the same area.

With appetites whetted and blood pressures slightly elevated, we began our tour at the prison's administration building, scene of the Rothe murder, a site at which orbs have been observed. The routine was simple. Enter an area where activity could be anticipated, sit, then wait and observe. While we were in the administration area, a sudden twelve-degree drop in temperature was recorded by an infrared thermometer. The temperature returned to normal again within seconds.

"That is generally agreed to be a sign of an unknown presence," Eric said.

The next stop, the main cellblock, included solitary-confinement cells, and the maximum-security cellblock, sites at which paranormal events have been recorded.

Kris said that the darkest region of the main cellblock had frightened him more than any other area of the prison. While we waited silently for some evidence of an unseen visitor, another tour member took a series of random photographs near cell number forty-six, a flash attachment illuminating the dark. When we viewed the photos on the camera's digital display, they clearly showed an orb about the size of a soccer ball directly over Julia's head. From that point on, everyone on the tour seemed to be walking on eggshells.

"Definitely something going on there," Kris concluded. He did not have to ask a second time if we were ready to move on.

After touring the maximum-security cellblock, we came to a cubicle attached to the exterior of the building, a site place where inmates had been allowed to receive visitors. The previous evening the exterior door had, without the aid of wind or human intervention, opened itself. And following the departure of tour members, lights that had been turned off were mysteriously turned on.

We experienced our own scary moment. As we stood outside the cellblock listening to Eric recall the previous night's events, we clearly heard the clanging of a closing metal cell door from deep inside the prison.

When three of us returned to the cellblock, we confirmed that there were no living humans inside. Eric had previously explained that this was the same cellblock in which voices had been recorded by ghosthunters from Seattle.

Undeterred by the unexplainable sounds, I returned to the cellblock with Patrick Straub, another member of the tour group, and Eric, who shot footage with his video camera. "We may be recording something, but will not see it until we play the video," he said.

Patrick did see something. Or thinks he did. "I just saw an orb at the lower corner of that cell," he said anxiously. "Or something like that."

After the stroke of midnight, on the anniversary of the riot's end, it was with great anticipation, and some apprehension, that we headed up the narrow, winding stairway to the fourth floor gun station from which Myles and Smart had departed this planet. After listening to Kris's patient attempts to arouse the spirits—"Is anyone here? Is there anything you want to say to us? Can you give us a sign?"—we concluded that, if there were any spirits in the area, they had taken the night off.

The Bratliens aren't the only ones investigating paranormal activity in Montana. Ellen Baumler comes to the subject as an historian. When asked to investigate the presence of a spirit in a home or other site, she apparently takes a skeptical, but open-minded, approach. Her approach is first to unearth the history of a property and its former occupants. If she can determine a possibility for paranormal presence based on historical fact, she forges ahead.

In her book, *Spirit Tailings,* her story, "The Body in the Bath-tub," serves as an excellent example. It seems as though a respected matron named Lucille lived alone in a large house in Virginia City from the 1940s until the 1980s. During the latter years of her occupancy, she had taken to rambling about a "horrific, bloody apparition that occasionally manifested itself" in her bathtub. She eventually became so irrational that the locals began referring to her as "Loose Wheel." Exhausted by the stress, she eventually sold the property and moved on.

The new owner did some sleuthing, however, and eventu-ally compiled a history of the house. Prior to Lucille's arrival, it seems that the house was owned by a married couple from Chicago. The husband was robbed and murdered by road agents. In 1905, after a second couple took ownership of the property, this husband also died and, following his death, the despondent widow committed suicide in the bathroom.

More than twenty similar stories are contained in the pages of Baumler's books, causing skeptics to pause before totally dis-counting the possibility of spirits. (An aside: Though she is reluc-tant to discuss the matter, the house in which the Baumler family resides has also been certified as having ethereal spirits within its confines.)

Other examples include the Crowne Plaza Hotel in Billings, formerly the Sheraton, where an elevator has been known to call the front desk for service at 2:30 A.M. However, neither the front desk manager or security guard has been able to learn who's making the call.

Chico Hot Springs Lodge and Resort is a Montana landmark. It combines the charm of an historic hotel with the environment of a hot springs and dude ranch. Some of its former guests were so taken with the place that they have, apparently, extended their visits past the grave. In May 1986, two night watchmen came upon the airy form of a young woman hovering near a piano in the third floor lounge. The face of the apparition lingered long enough to allow a guard to snap a photograph. As typically happens, when the film was processed, only a tiny white spot appeared. While this was not the first time the "Lady in White" had been seen, it was the first time that she had allowed herself to be photographed.

Four years later, two other guards followed the Lady from the lobby to the hallway leading to room 349, where her presence has been reported by many employees and guests. There's also a rocking chair in room 349 that, regardless of its initial location, eventually ends up facing a window.

In Virginia City, the Bonanza Inn was the first county courthouse in Virginia City but was replaced in 1876 and converted to a Catholic Hospital. Next door, Bonanza House was later converted to a nunnery. The ghost of a nun has appeared in both places. Furthermore, one room at the inn is now sealed because of a series of frightening poltergeist manifestations. The apparition of a lecherous man has appeared in one of the upstairs rooms at the Bonanza House. Mysterious footsteps, strange feelings of discomfort, and bone-chilling cold spots are common occurrences.

At Bannack State Park in Dillon, the park's assistant manager, Tom Lowe, has a ghost story of his own. It seems as though the residents of Bannack have an annual Halloween Walk. It's an opportunity for participants to paint their faces in a ghostly motif, dress up like the ladies and gentlemen who resided in the city in the 1860s, and generally have a grand time. In 2001, however, they discovered that they might not be alone. At the end of the evening's festivities, many of the participants gathered for a group photo. When Lowe had the film processed, he discovered that an uninvited image had barged into his viewfinder. "That's not a person, or a reflection from a bright object, or anything we can explain," he said. "It does look something like a ghost, doesn't it?"

Shirley Smith of Fromberg, in addition to being preoccupied with the Little People in the Pryors, is also the proprietress of the Little Cowboy Bar and Museum. During our first meeting, she casually mentioned the frequent appearance of Hank Deines, the former owner of the bar. Hank's presence in the bar continued for years after his death, and Ms. Smith wasn't the only recipient of his attention.

Hank, it seems, died in 1971 while lying on a cot in a back corner of the bar. Ms. Smith subsequently purchased the establishment from Hank's widow, Mary, who later moved to Billings. Hank's spirit, however, seems to have remained in Fromberg.

Ms. Smith recalled a disconcerting evening, "There were three customers sitting at the bar. I was filling glass mugs that hang on cup hooks on the wall with peanuts. They are on hooks, so very secure. All of a sudden, the cups flew up into the air, dislodged one of the ceiling tiles, and landed on the bar without breaking a mug!"

She continued, "An employee named Teaia was working the late shift and, while handling cleaning chores, was playing music very loudly. That apparently disturbed Hank because Teaia began hearing a dull pounding sound on one of the tables. When she ignored the sound, the pounding increased in tempo and velocity, at which point Teaia said, 'OK, Hank, I'll turn off the music.' She did, and the pounding stopped."

Hank's visits apparently stopped in 2003. "But he returned in 2006," Shirley said. "Or someone did." Light fixtures seemed to have taken on a life of their own. "They are turning themselves on and off. The same is true of some of the machines. . . . And our security guards have seen people in the building in the middle of the night, long after we've closed and the place is empty. Is it Hank? It could be him, or someone else who likes the place. Whoever it is, I kind of like having him around because, so far, he's been harmless."

Considering the number of level-headed, educated Montanans who have had experiences with the paranormal, it's hard to ignore the possibility that we might share our space with the dead. So the next time a teacup falls from the mantle for no apparent reason or the dogs start howling, you might want to reach for the video recorder. Or at least find a safe spot under the sofa.

EPILOGUE

A SHAGGY DOG STORY PRODUCES A MYSTERY

So there you have it, a smattering of mysteries and legends from the Treasure State. Given the number of sightings of Unidentified Flying Objects, we have to wonder: Is Montana's famous Big Sky filled with more than commercial, recreational, or military aircraft? And what about Harry Plummer? Was he an honest sheriff wrongfully murdered or was he himself the leader of a gang of bandits? And if he was crooked, where did he hide his loot? Then there's the mysterious death of the former governor, General Meagher, in Fort Benton. Did a sick man fall overboard while answering the call of nature or did he kill himself? Or was he the victim of Vigilantes? And what about paranormal spirits? It becomes increasingly difficult to argue against their existence, especially since so many people who have no connection with each other have experiences with uninvited guests. If you're a skeptic, spend an evening with the Bratliens during a midnight tour of the Old Prison, and you might be surprised at how your thinking can change. Then there are all those incidents relating to the Little People, to Flessie, and to Bigfoot. And we're just getting warmed up.

So we'll add one more, a mystery that involves a sheep dog named Shep, who spent the final years of his life in Fort Benton where so much of Montana's history took place.

The mystery dates to 1936, when Shep arrived in town in the company of his master, a sheepherder who fell ill while tending his flock. The sick sheepherder was lodged at St. Clare Hospital, but no thought was given to his companion, a furry black-and-white canine. While awaiting the release of his master, Shep loitered for days, waiting patiently at the hospital door. One kind nun who ran the kitchen occasionally fed him a plate of leftovers.

Following the death of the sheepherder, family members apparently requested that his body be shipped east by railcar. On an August day, Shep watched as an undertaker rolled a gurney bearing a casket across the station platform where it was loaded aboard the luggage car. Attendants at the station recall that Shep was so distressed that he began whining when the door was slammed shut and the train slowly departed the station. They also describe the distraught pup trotting briefly down the tracks after the train. Certain that his master would return, Shep went back to the station and began a five-and-a-half-year vigil.

He became a fixture on the platform, and the unofficial greeter of the four trains that arrived at the station every day. He stood watching as passengers dismounted, hoping for the arrival of his master. At first he was chased away by the railroad employees; but he eventually became their ward, and they provided him with food and shelter.

As word of his vigil spread across the land, Shep attained celebrity status. In 1938 he was featured in *Ripley's Believe It or Not,* and rail travelers reportedly took long detours off the main line to stop in Fort Benton. Shep began receiving fan mail from school children and gifts at Christmas.

Sadly, the aging process and cold winters took their toll on the pup. He became stiff legged and hard of hearing and, on January 12, 1942, failed to hear the roar of engine number 235 as it rolled into the station at 10:17 A.M. The engine was almost upon Shep— and he was moving out of its way—when he slipped on the icy rails, and his long watch ended. His death also altered the life of the train's engineer, who refused to drive the Fort Benton route again.

The following day, news of Shep's death and an obituary were carried on the wires of the Associated Press and United Press International. With hundreds of mourners in attendance, a Boy Scout honor guard carried a pine box containing the remains of Fort Benton's famous citizen to a burial plot on a lonely bluff overlooking the train depot. The Great Northern Railroad erected a simple obelisk, with a painted wooden cutout of Shep next to it. Beneath it, white stones spelled out SHEP. Lights illuminated the display at night, and conductors pointed it out to their passengers. Eventually, though, the passenger line stopped coming through Fort Benton, and the grave fell into disrepair.

Then, of course, there's "The Rest of the Story."

Perhaps enlightened by a mention Paul Harvey made of the dog in 1988, a new generation of Shep fans was born. A group of admirers banded together to repair and refurbish Shep's grave, replace the wooden cutout with a painted steel monument, and restore the lights. A small parking area and walking trail were also created. For the fiftieth anniversary of Shep's death, the community of Fort Benton organized a committee to produce a lasting memorial to their famous dog. Using photos of Shep, Montanan Bob Scriver, perhaps the most famous bronze sculptor in the West, created a larger than life-sized statue of the town's famous mutt.

Today, at a peaceful, shady site on the levee in the center of town, Shep's likeness continues its vigil at Shepherd's Court, now the town's focal point. His collar and food dish are nearby on display in the Museum of the Upper Missouri where historian Ken Robison responds to the frequent requests for photos and information. "Within the past year at least a dozen authors have contacted the Overholser Historical Research Center," said Robison. In early 2006, newly elected Governor Brian Schweitzer requested two photos of Shep, which now hang in his office.

In 2005, out of the blue, unsolicited photos of the famous dog began finding their way to Robison. Lindsay Duckett provided a photo of Shep that was taken along the Great Northern tracks. Irene Schanche Boker, whose father Tony Schanche was station agent during the dog's vigil, provided twenty newly dis-

OVERHOLSEN HISTORICAL RESEARCH CENTER

One of Montana's most famous pets, Shep became a well-known and beloved figure at the Fort Benton train platform.

covered photos. And Fred Arnst donated a DVD with 16mm film coverage of Shep taken in 1940.

The mystery? Well, it doesn't amount to much.

Though he is but a minor player in this drama, the identity of Shep's owner is a missing piece in the tale. Historian Robison said he may have been one of two sheepherders who died in the mid-1930s, except their bodies are in a nearby cemetery while Shep's owner's body was shipped back east. Or he may have been one of three cowboys who died and were shipped to points east and south. "I am still trying to determine the sheepherder's identity," Robison said.

You've heard and seen the chronicles of brave and loyal companions like Lassie, Rin Tin Tin, and Old Yeller dramatized in radio and television. But Shep's was a drama played out in real life, the heartbreaking and heartwarming elements accentuated by a little bit of mystery. Like most of Montana's enduring narratives, it's been enough to capture our imaginations all these years later.

BIBLIOGRAPHY

What Happened to Meriwether's Boat?

Camp, Carl, "Journey's End for the Iron Boat," in *We Proceeded On*. Lewis and Clark Trail Heritage Foundation, August 2003.

Jackson, Donald. *The Letters of the Lewis and Clark Expedition with Related Documents*. Champaign: University of Illinois Press, 1979.

Moulton, Gary E. *The Definitive Journals of Lewis and Clark*. Lincoln: University of Nebraska Press, 1993.

A Mummy and the Little People

Clark, Ella E. *Indian Legends from the Northern Rockies*. Norman: University of Oklahoma Press, 1966.

Murray, Earl. *Ghosts of the Old West.* New York: Tor Books, 1998.

"The Pedro Mountain Mummy." *The Casper Star-Tribune,* July 22, July 24, 1979.

"The Pedro Mountain Mummy." *The Casper Tribune Herald,* October 22, 1932.

Pittsley, Rich. "Little People: Dressed Like Elvis." *The Billings Outpost,* July 3, 2002.

Smith, Shirley. "The Little People," n.p.

Did Governor Meagher Go Swimming?
Or Was He Drowned?

"Accident or Suicide?" *The Eureka Journal,* January 26,1928.

"Account of the Drowning of Gen. Thomas Francis Meagher," in *Contributions to the Historical Society of Montana: Volume 8.* S. Canner and Company, 1966. 131.

Athearn, Robert G. *Thomas Francis Meagher: An Irish Revolutionary in America.* Boulder: University of Colorado Press, 1949.

"The Death of Gen. Thomas Francis Meagher." *Helena Tri-Weekly,* July 6, 1867.

Stevens, Christian D. *Meagher of the Sword*. New York: Mead and Company, 1967.

Was Frank Little Murdered by a Cop?

Axline, Jonathan A. "This is a case for the police." Master's thesis, Montana State University, June 1985.

State of Montana. Certificate of Death, Edward Morrissey. February 6, 1922.

Walter, Dave, ed. *Speaking Ill of the Dead*. Guilford, Conn.: Globe Pequot Press, 2000.

"Who Killed Frank Little?" *Anaconda Standard*, February 2, 1922.

Is the Mystery of the Easton Murder Solved?

"Prolific Robber Found Dead." *The Spokesman-Review*, February 8, 2001.

Was Sheriff Henry Plummer a Highway Robber?

Allen, Frederick. *A Decent, Orderly Hanging*. Norman: University of Oklahoma Press, 2004.

Baumler, Ellen. *Beyond Spirit Tailings.* Helena: Montana Historical Society Press, 2005.

Langford, Nathaniel. *Vigilante Days and Ways.* New York: Grosset and Dunlap, Inc., 1890.

Mather, R. E., and F. E. Boswel. *Hanging the Sheriff.* Salt Lake City: University of Utah Press, 1987.

Is There a Connection Between UFOs and Cattle Mutilations?

"Cattle mutilations back: Ranchers, lawmen baffled by crime wave." *Great Falls Tribune,* January 3, 2002.

Donovan, Roberta, and Keith Wolverton. *Mystery Stalks the Prairies.* Raynesford, Mont.: T.H.A.R. Institute, 1976.

National Institute for Discovery Science. "Summary Report on a Wave of UFO/Helicopters and Animal Mutilations in Cascade County, Montana, 1974–1977." Las Vegas, 2002.

If Bigfoot Exists, He Needs a Shower . . .

Big Foot Research Organization database. www.bfro.net.

"Commissioner candidate says he's seen a Bigfoot." *The Hungry Horse News,* May 18, 2006.

Donovan, Roberta, and Keith Wolverton. *Mystery Stalks the Prairies.* Raynesford, Mont.: T.H.A.R. Institute, 1976.

"Is Bigfoot roaming around Kiowa Camp in Blackfeet Country?" *The Glacier Reporter,* March 2, 2006.

"Professor Bigfoot." *Associated Press,* November 4, 2006.

Who Named the Crazy Mountains?

"The Crazy Mountains." Crazy Mountain Museum pamphlet.

Fisher, Vardis. *Mountain Man.* Moscow, Idaho: University of Idaho Press, 1965.

Linderman, Frank Bird, and Plenty-Coups. *Plenty Coups: Chief of the Crows.* Lincoln: University of Nebraska Press, 2002.

"Long on Beauty, Rich in History." *Big Timber Pioneer,* July 9, 1993.

Van Cleve, Spike. *Forty Years' Gatherin's.* Kansas City: Lowell Press, 1977.

Meet Flessie, the Monster of Flathead Lake

Baumler, Ellen. *Beyond Spirit Tailings.* Helena: Montana Historical Society Press, 2002.

Fugleberg, Paul. *Montana Nessie of Flathead Lake.* Polson, Mont.: Treasure State Publishing, 1992.

"Two New Reports of Flathead Monster Surface." *Bigfork Eagle,* August 11, 2005.

"What Are Your Chances of Sighting the Monster?" Laney Hanzel, *Flathead Lake Monitor,* July 1995.

There Are Ghosts in the Butte Archives, Aren't There?

Baumler, Ellen. *Spirit Tailings.* Helena: Montana Historical Society Press, 2005.

Bratlien, Eric. "Investigations: Old Montana Prison," Tortured Souls Investigations Web site: www.tsimt.net.

Erickson, Martin. "Someone To Love Me." Self-published pamphlet.

"Haunted Places in Montana." theshadowlands.net/places/ montana.htm.

A Shaggy Dog Story Produces a Mystery

The Story of Shep. Fort Benton: The River Press, n.d.

INDEX

ABOUT THE AUTHOR

Ed Lawrence is a writer and photographer based in Bozeman, Montana. He combines his passion for flyfishing with work for major magazines. He is also the author of *Frommer's Guide to Montana and Wyoming* and *Frommer's Guide to Yellowstone and Grand Teton National Parks.*